"Paul Ricoeur would no doubt rejoice! This lively account and appreciation of the sacred in the profane, the extraordinary in the ordinary, is not unlike the parables of Jesus and as such provides a wonderful model for theological reflection. Mary's account of events and relationships have a matter of fact quality giving way to a deep appreciation and the profound influence of Benedict in chartering her way through life. Particularly poignant is her honest account experienced in the transition from an appointment as prioress back to her cherished teaching. Dashed expectations and the whirlpool of confusion chiselling out a greater connectedness to reality and to new life."

> — Marie Biddle, SJ
> Coordinator of Spirituality Programs
> Aquinas Academy, Sydney, Australia

"In my book, *Meditation in Motion*, I remind readers to 'resolve at least for today to become aware of the many openings to prayer provided by ordinary reality.' Needless to say, I congratulate the author of this book, a former student of mine, for helping her readers to re-appreciate the richness embedded in everyday life. She counsels us all to live on that razor's edge between time and eternity and to see with new eyes what we might otherwise have missed."

> — Susan Muto, PhD
> Dean, Epiphany Academy of Formative Spirituality

"In her inspired and indispensable book, S. Mary Reuter gives new meaning to 'common sense:' she teaches us how to employ all our senses in understanding the seemingly common and discover deep spiritual meaning in the everyday."

> — Martha Tomhave Blauvelt
> College of St. Benedict
> Collegeville, Minnesota

"*Running with Expanded Heart* offers a vision of how the spirituality of Saint Benedict can provide inspiration and guidance for 21st-century Christians—including the laity. Mary Reuter understands just how down-to-earth and practical Benedictine wisdom is and uses storytelling, personal reflection, and thought-provoking open-ended questions to illustrate just how relevant Benedict's Rule continues to be. Beginning with an homage to her father whom she describes as an 'extraordinary ordinary man,' Reuter goes on to show, in a variety of ways, how Benedictine wisdom can help Christians to find the extraordinary in all of life's ordinary moments. This book can serve both as an introduction to Benedictine spirituality for beginners, but also as a bouquet of new insights for those who have walked with Benedict for some time."

> — Carl McColman
> Blogger (www.anamchara...
> Author of *The Big Book of Christian Mysticism*

W9-BWU-998

"Drawing on wisdom that has been slowly ripened in the rhythms of monastic stability, Benedictine Mary Reuter reveals the way she has grown into her own expanding heart by sharing engaging personal stories with which any one of us can easily identify. The words and stories discovered in *Running with Expanding Heart: Meeting God in Everyday Life* may be deceptively simple, but they illuminate the ultimately mysterious nooks and crannies of the human soul and encourage us to attend to the Spirit gently moving through the moments of our ordinary days."

— Wendy M. Wright, PhD
Professor of Theology, Creighton University

"Mining and minding the moment becomes thoughtfully exhilarating as Sister Mary provides a respectful look at the unfolding presence of God in daily life. Guided by her insights, her stories, her own vulnerability and her sharing of Scripture and the Rule of Benedict, readers gain ways to develop a pattern for strengthening and expanding their hearts as they discover God in life's experiences. Like supportive running shoes, each chapter takes one forward on the path of life."

— Michaela Hedican, OSB
Prioress
Saint Bede Monastery
Eau Claire, Wisconsin

"*Running with Expanding Heart* shows amazing and even startling stories of where, when, how to find God in everyday life. Mary's creativity opens new vistas when she invites us to consider 'finding a pearl in the salad dressing' or finding God in a world that is '. . . studded and strewn with pennies.' Having been introduced by Sr. Mary to the image of the 'Walking Madonna' years ago reminded me of her incredible ability to discover God in the difficult moments as well as the jubilee moments of her life. This creative endeavor of Sister Mary Reuter's highlights her love of her Benedictine roots, her love of the Gospel and for all little ones and searchers of our world. A 'must' read for all who wish to *run with an expanding heart*!"

— Sister Eleanor Granger, OSF
Sisters of Saint Francis
Rochester, Minnesota

"Reuter reminds us with embarrassingly accurate detail that the intrusions and interruptions we grit teeth and grind jaws over can be, to the attentive, invitations from God who, once we offer a nod of permission, is ready to re-order our day toward the divine. Hers is a perennial and timely message for our lives that are so ruled by the immediacy of the internet."

— Larry Lewis, M.M.
author of *The Misfit-Haunting the Human Unveiling the Divine*

Running with Expanding Heart
Meeting God in Everyday Life

Mary Reuter, OSB

Foreword by Patrick Henry

LITURGICAL PRESS
Collegeville, Minnesota

www.litpress.org

Cover design by Ann Blattner. Photo: iStockphoto.com.

John O'Donohue, "A Blessing," from *Eternal Echoes: Exploring Our Yearning to Belong.* Copyright © 1999 by John O'Donohue. Reprinted by permission of HarperCollins Publishers.

Gerard Manley Hopkins, "God's Grandeur," in *Gerard Manley Hopkins*, edited by Catherine Phillips. Copyright © 1995. Reprinted by permission of Oxford University Press on behalf of The British Province of the Society of Jesus.

Excerpts from *Being Home: Discovering the Spiritual in the Everyday,* by Gunilla Norris. Copyright © 1991, 2001 by Gunilla Norris. Hidden Spring, an imprint of Paulist Press, Inc., New York/Mahwah, NJ. Reprinted by permission of Paulist Press, Inc. www.paulistpress.com.

Scripture texts in this work are taken from the *New Revised Standard Version Bible: Catholic Edition* © 1989, 1993, Division of Christian Education of the National Council of the Churches of Christ in the United States of America. Used by permission. All rights reserved.

1   2   3   4   5   6   7   8   9

Library of Congress Cataloging-in-Publication Data

Reuter, Mary.
    Running with expanding heart : meeting God in everyday life /
Mary Reuter ; foreword by Patrick Henry.
        p. cm.
    Includes bibliographical references (p.   ).
    ISBN 978-0-8146-3308-3 — ISBN 978-0-8146-3920-7 (e-book)
  1. Christian life—Catholic authors.   I. Title.

    BX2350.3.R48 2010
    248.4'82—dc22   2009051935

To my family,
especially Mom and Dad,
and to my Benedictine community
who have taught me that *ordinary time*
and all that happens during it
are sacred and can be lived as praise of God.

Contents

Foreword

by Patrick Henry

Once upon a time, 900 years ago, the line between the monastery and the "outside" world was fuzzy. In the twenty books of her delightful Brother Cadfael mystery series, novelist Ellis Peters demonstrates repeatedly how many contacts monastic folk and common folk had with each other. The monastery was a community center, the hub of civic activity.

There is certainly much that is different between our time and the Middle Ages, but one thing we have in common is an indistinct border between monasteries and the world. By this I do not mean that the twelfth and twenty-first centuries are secularized corruptions of an original monastic ideal. On the contrary, St. Benedict and other founders were committed to healing the world, not escaping from it.

In very broad strokes, this sets the scene for Sister Mary's book. I am fortunate to know well both Mary and her community, Saint Benedict's Monastery in Saint Joseph, Minnesota. It would be hard to find anywhere a group of people more alert to current events, to the hurts and joys of their neighbors, whether next door or on the other side of the world. Their core values— Awareness of God, Community, Prayer and Work, Listening, Hospitality, Stewardship, Peace—taken straight from the Rule of Benedict, mark the territory they claim for their mission. There is no member of the human family they classify as alien, no part of the planet they consider foreign.

In the popular imagination, monastics are sometimes an amalgam of sanctity and silliness, as in many movies where they are by turns pious and naive. Occasionally their cleverness is portrayed, as when the sisters in *The Sound of Music* outwit the Nazis by pulling wires from a car's engine. But I suspect that most people, until recently, figured that those who live in monasteries wouldn't have much practical advice to offer.

In my lifetime, now beginning its eighth decade, I have witnessed many spiritual revolutions. One of the most profound (and surprising) has been the growing attention to monastics, and to monastic traditions more generally, as a source of practical insight that is practical precisely because it is grounded in a clear, unsentimental, but ultimately hopeful understanding of human nature. People are discovering that those who live in monasteries have something a friend of mine once called "a spirituality for the long haul"—and since we're all in the long haul together, we'd better pay attention to those who have reckoned how to make the best of it.

Running with Expanding Heart: Meeting God in Everyday Life takes its place in a growing library of wisdom literature that includes Thomas Merton, OCSO; Joan Chittister, OSB; Mary Margaret Funk, OSB; David Steindl-Rast, OSB; Sister Jeremy Hall, OSB (late of Saint Benedict's Monastery); and many others.

Kathleen Norris has alerted hundreds of thousands of readers to what she has learned about the depth and breadth of life in her encounters—some brief, some extended over many years—with sons and daughters of St. Benedict and his twin sister, St. Scholastica. And here is something Norris has noticed, and so have I: the Benedictine commitment to community, far from homogenizing monastics into indistinguishable holiness, produces people of stunning uniqueness.

Sister Mary Reuter makes her own inimitable contribution to the library of Benedictine wisdom literature. The point of her book is to prompt you to be alert to how God is there to be met in *your* everyday life, your unique everyday life.

You probably haven't had a moment of revelation when you dropped a salad dressing bottle and it broke, and a similar occasion might very well not get your attention as it did Sister Mary's.

But once you know what she learned from it, how it brought her face up against some habits that soured her spirit and diminished her effectiveness, you will be more ready to let God get through to you when you do something hasty or stupid.

"Dad seemed so ordinary he could easily be overlooked." Maybe this is not your dad, but it was Mary's, and the insights she gained from talking to people at his funeral might sharpen your alertness so you won't "overlook" God's image that other people are. Benedict "realizes that people are drowsy, going through their daily routine in habits that keep them comfortable and unaware of what's going on within and outside them." Mary has found that Benedict is right: if we're awake, really awake, we'll discover that God is lurking around nearly every corner, "hidden behind what we perceive."

A monastic practice that attracts a lot of popular interest is one called *lectio divina*, a slow, ruminative reading of texts, usually from the Bible, in which the point is not to solve an intellectual puzzle but to let the text get under your skin and start to read you more than you read it. Mary is especially adept at this with the parables of Jesus, and she shows us not only the parables she has discovered in her own life but also how all of us can "serve as initiators and supporters of parables in the lives of others." She is grateful to those who have been such initiators and supporters for her, who have given her "deep roots to support [her] life and branches to reach out to others."

I suspect you will find much of what you read in these pages staying with you because what Mary knows is grounded in stories, and stories are what we remember. We also (I anyway) remember insights that sneak up, that mingle shrewdness and humor. Mary's analysis of the way we talk about time—we mark it, spend it, kill it, run out of it, waste it, are just a few of the metaphors she notices—startled me, and maybe will make me more hospitable toward time, befriending it, as Mary suggests, not competing against it.

You may have suspected, as I did a long time ago, that monastic folks are more straitjacketed than the rest of us; after all, they live a life of discipline, they follow a Rule. But Sister Mary makes clear that one fruit of the disciplined life is, paradoxically, a heightened ability to choose. Over and over again in these pages she reminds us that we can—must—make choices about how we interpret the things that happen to us and that we make happen. I don't have to react; I can respond. And Mary knows this can be really tough. She takes us through a period of several months when she was faced with disillusionment and disorientation.

Sister Mary, paraphrasing Gail Godwin, says that our lives can keep on making more of us. This is a pretty good summary of Benedictine wisdom and reflects the truth embedded in the title of the book, right out of the Rule of Benedict—*Running with Expanding Heart*. I daresay this is a truth that Brother Cadfael and his contemporaries in the twelfth century understood. We are lucky that Sister Mary Reuter and her contemporaries—you and I—in the twenty-first century are rediscovering it.

Patrick Henry lives in Waite Park, Minnesota, and retired in 2004 after twenty years as executive director of the Collegeville Institute for Ecumenical and Cultural Research. Previously he was professor of religion at Swarthmore College. He is author of *The Ironic Christian's Companion: Finding the Marks of God's Grace in the World* and, with Donald Swearer, *For the Sake of the World: The Spirit of Buddhist and Christian Monasticism*.

Preface

Some would call Leo, my dad, a custom tractor worker, but as a child I considered him to be a magician with a little Ford tractor. It seemed Dad and his tractor could do whatever he envisioned, as any artist can. He dug post holes for building barns and plowed gardens for planting in the spring. When a snowstorm blew in, I could hear the drone of his tractor by 3:00 a.m. as he left home to plow snow out of driveways and parking lots in our small town, making it possible for people to get to work and school on snowy days. In spring he plowed gardens for people who later watched in hopeful anticipation of vegetables and fruits. During the summer Dad dug basements that would serve as the foundation for new homes. Later he came back to landscape the yards to designer perfection. The partners, Dad and his tractor, worked well together. They also had fun. Many times they pulled my siblings and me on exciting toboggan rides out in the open spaces near our home.

With this brief introduction to Dad, I move to the events of his wake and funeral in 1970. Through them my eyes were opened wide, and I could see with new lenses. It was at that time I received the effects of Dad's magic. I became more sensitive to the value of ordinary events in my life that I previously had overlooked.

Dad was intent on living with a gospel heart. Thus, he looked to Jesus for ways to live his calling as a Christian, and Jesus served him well. Jesus is also here for us.

St. Benedict of Nursia (480–547) provides a guide, the Rule of Benedict, for Christians who are called to live the gospel as monastics.[1] They live within a specifically designed structure, with special focus on Christ and some of his values expressed in the gospel and with emphasis on some practices that can form the heart and influence its expression. A gift of St. Benedict's guide is its applicability for any Christian's life. It draws from the wisdom he gained through his life journey, first as a hermit and then as he lived with and guided monks in the monasteries he established. In exploring ways that daily events offer opportunities to meet and respond to God, I note some of the principles and practices St. Benedict includes in his guide, especially those that focus on everyday life. St. Benedict also points out that "our hearts expand" as we advance in living as a disciple of Christ, as we stretch our hearts when we run "the way of God's commandments with love."[2] This wisdom echoes the invitation of Jesus who says to all of us, "Follow me," by loving in attitude and actions (Matt 4:19).

This book draws from experiences—my own, those of others, and those of people in Scripture and other literature. I invite you to let the examples evoke your own experiences. This book is not for me. It is for you, to expand your vision and heart so you can love more fully through your own daily events.

I suggest some practices you might use in your own life. I include questions to draw you into reflection. However, this book is not a "how to" text. I refrain from extensive descriptions of formative practices. I include the thinking of some wise people so you hear their voice of guidance. Also, sources noted in the endnotes and bibliography can lead you to further resources.

My dad awaits you in Chapter 1. Other people will walk with you through the pages of this book. The chapters focus on some of the values St. Benedict stressed: the view that everything is holy; hospitality; obedience (listening, discerning, and responding); stability; *conversatio* (structures and practices that support a change of heart and actions in daily events); and dramatic experiences. As you consider and value more fully the stuff of your daily life, expect blessings to be lurking in occurrences that might seem minor or that you have overlooked. I trust you will find that St. Benedict's hope will become a fuller reality in your everyday experiences: "so that in all things God may be glorified" (RB 57:9 [1 Pet 4:11]).

I hope you will become much more aware of the miracles in your lives. According to a Jewish perspective, miracles are any events "in which one sees the power and love of God."[3] We know that miracles are God's doing, but they also depend on us, the ones who, with the help of God, are attentive and who notice.[4] I hope that as you read this book, you will see more miracles in your daily life and will live with deeper faith that God loves you unconditionally and constantly. I hope, too, that your life will continue to grow into a well-practiced prayer of joy, gratitude, and praise.

Acknowledgments

My gratitude goes to my family, especially Mom and Dad, who first modeled the importance of giving attention to encounters of daily life. I thank my Benedictine sisters for their influence in expanding my heart and in maturing my ability to live according to the principles given by Christ and later by St. Benedict of Nursia. I am grateful particularly for the example of their lives—lives that have taught me how to live a life of compassion and service.

I am grateful to Studium, the Scholars-in-Residence program at Saint Benedict's Monastery, for the space and resources that helped me step apart during my sabbatical to begin writing this book. Gratitude also goes to the faculty of the Institute of Formative Spirituality at Duquesne University for their guidance during my doctoral work: Adrian Van Kaam, CSSp, Susan Muto, Carolyn Gratton, Charles Maes, and Richard Byrne, OCSO. Thank you to Diane Millis and Lynn Bye, who served as writing partners during the early stages of this book. And to the many people along the way who have read and given feedback on parts of the manuscript, thank you; some can witness to the many shavings left behind as the book has been whittled into the shape it has become. Special thanks go to Stefanie Weisgram, OSB, who has read and reread versions of the text and found some of the resources I needed. I thank Scott Russell Sanders, who recognized vitality in what I was writing; his voice served as encouragement when I became tired of it all. Thank you to Marie Biddle, SJ, for the use of her photo of the "Two Madonnas" in Salisbury, England. My gratitude goes to Marold Kornovich, OSB, whose contemporary psalm gives us some of her wisdom gained during her ninety-three years of living with a gradually expanding heart. Thank you to Sylvia Sultenfuss for her reflection that highlights some of her surprises as she moved through an ordinary day, allowing it to reveal the extraordinary.

I am grateful, too, to the students and participants in workshops and retreats I have facilitated; their responses and commitment to their faith journeys have convinced me that the topic of this book needs to be explored so people can be open to their daily experiences with respect and expectation of blessings. I am especially grateful to the monks of Subiaco Abbey, Arkansas, whose invitation to present some reflections during a retreat has resulted in the chapters of this book.

I note readers, each of whom brought her perspective to the subject matter and writing style: Roberta Bondi, Rosalie Klimisch, Julia Ahlers Ness, Carol Johannes (whose eye for detailed editing could win her employment by any publisher), Martha Tomhave Blauvelt (who has already found herself in chapter 6), and Sylvia Sultenfuss (who has been a constant cheerleader and continually reminded me that this book needs to be written). And I thank Patrick Henry for his foreword; he "gets it" regarding my monastic community and the importance of daily parables available to every person. I also thank him for his editing that has given the reflections greater clarity.

I thank the staff of Liturgical Press for its expertise and gracious service. I note especially Mary Stommes, whose editing skills have become an art and who knows well how to serve as a companion to an author who needs to move through revisions and learn necessary "how to's." And thanks, too, to Ann Blattner, who sifted through several options for the cover and persevered with me as I discerned the focus and design.

Chapter 1

Everything Is Holy

. . . the ineffable inhabits the magnificent and the common,
the grandiose and the tiny facts of reality alike.[1]

An Extraordinary Ordinary Man

October 5, 1970, started as an ordinary teaching day. A phone call from my brother Roger changed everything. "Mary, Dad just died of a heart attack." Thus began days of encounters that opened my eyes wide. I caught glimpses of Dad that I had not seen or given much attention to. As I walked through Dad's wake and funeral, I was plunged into awareness and reflection that would affect deeply who I was and how I would live in the following years. Little did I realize then how much my heart would expand, a change that would be irrevocable.

Dad was only sixty years old. His sudden death stunned everyone. During his wake, people stood in a long line outside the mortuary and gradually made their way to the casket to say good-bye. People kept coming, weeping, giving their condolences to my family, and sharing their memories of Dad, even as we consoled them. I noticed the stories about Dad's jokes, chats, compassion, and gift for creating beauty. With his Ford tractor he had plowed people's gardens in the spring, terraced lawns during the summer, and plowed snow out of driveways and school parking lots during the winter. These were Dad's tasks. But there was more.

Dad was a simple and unassuming man. On first glance, nothing significant marked his encounters with people. However, a second look revealed the influence of his simplicity, candor, and willingness to give something beyond the job he had been asked to do. Dad seemed so ordinary he could easily be overlooked. Yet his contagious spirit influenced many people. He was daily and ordinary, and yet so extraordinary.

I left Dad's wake and funeral with my heart tight. While weighed down with grief, I took home a heart full of stories and humor that had been exercised pulse by pulse through each person I'd met during those days of mourning and celebration. I also carried with me some questions: What lessons had Dad taught me throughout my life, even while I did not realize I was learning them? What lessons was I to learn from him now?

Dad reached out to people as part of his ordinary life. He soothed his crying children in the middle of the night; over the years he washed many baby bottles for his nine children. His lap welcomed little ones as a favorite place for rest and cuddling. We often heard stories from Dad's work activities. We learned about our aunts and uncles through tales of their childhood. Sunday afternoons gave us fun time with Dad as he played 500 Rummy with us. At times he'd interrupt the game to dance around the living room with my mother, in step with the ump-pa-pa of the old-time music on the radio. I recall Dad's special care during Christmas vacations when he'd warm the car before the family piled in and we'd set out to visit our grandparents, aunts, uncles, and cousins. Dad faithfully cheered on my brothers at their football and basketball games. Birthdays, weddings, births and baptisms of grandchildren, and funerals of relatives and friends all held honored places in his life. When he put on his dark suit with a white shirt and tie, he was transformed into a man of dignity while retaining his comfortable presence as Dad.

Dad, a shy man, took center stage for a scene in the play *Everyman*, presented by our local parish. Fear gradually loosened its hold on him as he publicly risked taking on a new identity for a few weeks. Dad was a man of deep feelings, even though those who did not know him well probably thought him to be quite reserved and unexpressive. He felt more comfortable keeping his feelings to himself than expressing them. However, I recall how they erupted into sobs when he received the news that his mother had died. He allowed himself to be held, vulnerable and unashamed, by my mother in his grief. Until then—as a fourteen-year-old—I had thought that men did not cry. Dad taught me otherwise.

Prayer regularly punctuated Dad's life. He took for granted that we prayed the rosary as a family during the months of Mary: May and October. Groans from my brothers could not deter this regular ritual after supper. Sundays, along with weekdays during Lent, were church-going occasions for the whole family. Every night we children could hear Dad and Mom pray their nighttime prayers together.

Even when he was very busy, Dad put quality, artistry, and people before expediency and efficiency. He took pride in a job done well. Often he interrupted his work to listen to people's stories about themselves and their families. Sometimes he slipped into stores to visit with friends when he passed by on his way to a work site. He often granted extensions to people he worked for who were having a hard time financially. Special sensitivity went to the elderly and disabled. In the winter it was his regular practice to sneak in and plow snow from a driveway in the dark, early hours of the morning without charging for the service. At the same time his sense of justice became provoked when a customer was unwilling to make the payment he had originally agreed upon.

Dad's death and what I learned about the value of ordinary encounters nudged me into remembering and reflecting on my childhood experiences and questions. I became aware that I had been intrigued for a long time with ordinary events and their influence on people's lives. As a child I was told that God meets us in our daily experiences. How would this happen? Would I hear a voice? Would I see someone? I hoped not. I'd be terrified. And people might think I was strange if I told them I saw God or I heard God talk to me.

Although I did not have the language for it in 1970, Dad's life and death taught me many lessons about the richness and vitality of a sacramental experience: God meets us and touches our lives in the midst of our daily experiences. I began to understand that conversion, the turning of our heart and actions to the attitudes and actions of Jesus, occurs gradually and often goes unnoticed. Daily events exercise our hearts, much as workouts strengthen our muscles. The process appears simple at first glance, but it is not easy in practice. Living a Christian life with its daily invitations and demands is not for the fainthearted. Furthermore, we need guidance to make our way through all the messages and openings we receive.

Where can we find wisdom to guide us? Over the years I have found two sources especially helpful. One is the gospel, where we can learn about Christ's perspective and actions, and the other is the Rule of Benedict of Nursia that outlines one way to live the gospel.

Jesus—A Celebrator of Ordinary Time

The gospels reveal the life and wisdom of Jesus Christ and his efforts to get people to think about the ultimate meaning of life. He both taught and modeled this meaning, showing us that the reign of God's love is lived here and now, not only in some future time of full glory. Jesus respected encounters with persons, things and events; he trusted that they could be life-giving. For example, when in his daily travels Jesus met people who were diseased, blind, and lame, he looked at them with compassion. He spoke to them. He touched them. People's lives were transformed. They saw, they walked, and they ran to tell others what had happened. Their hearts were changed, opening in gratitude and praise. As Jesus' heart expanded with care and as he acted out of this love, people were healed and returned to life.

Jesus involved himself in the usual tasks and encounters of his daily life. Ordinary things and gestures served as ways of giving life, of celebrating what we might consider ordinary time.

He broke bread and people were fed. Jesus touched the eyes of a blind man and he could see. From noticing how a seed sprouts and grows, he learned about the dying-rising pattern of life. He taught these insights to the people. Yeast and bread dough, mustard trees, and a woman looking for a lost coin became some of the bases of his parables. Jesus' familiarity with seeds and types of soil gave him images for stories that urged the listeners to cultivate their inner soil to receive life-shifting messages and to nurture growth. Jesus interacted with relatives and friends; he experienced hospitality. He also found himself in the middle of a family conflict about who had the better part, Martha busy providing food for guests or Mary sitting and listening to Jesus. Again, life taught him how to welcome guests, to love persons in ways unique to each, and to live creatively within the dynamic tension of activity and solitude. Might Jesus' involvement with the stuff of life encourage us to value more our own daily lives? Might he also give us the foresight to expect blessings from encounters that, at first glance, seem of little consequence?

In contrast to Jesus, we instinctively look for what is extraordinary and dramatic. None of us wants our life to be only a whimper. Daily situations often seem too mundane, too insignificant in the big scheme of things, and too fleeting to be important. However, dads, moms, friends, teachers, and business people doing everyday activities bring God's love to people they meet, providing openings through which the Spirit breathes into the world; they give opportunities for Christ to continue engaging in ordinary life situations. Really? And do these people together really pulse the vitality of the Body of Christ? Do ordinary people who are trying, struggling, and failing continue Jesus' dying and rising? Yes! How extraordinary!

St. Benedict's Perspective

St. Benedict of Nursia heard Jesus' message that the reign of God's love is here and now, not only in the past or the future. He centers his spirituality on the person of Jesus Christ. This

focus casts light on the place of daily life as monastics seek God
and put the love of Christ before all else (RB 58:7; 4:21). The
events of everyday life offer opportunities for us to die to our
own self-centeredness and to rise to fuller life with God and
God's concerns.[2] Christ is embodied and received in guests regardless of societal rank (RB 53:7), in the poor (RB 53:15), in
the sick (RB 36:1), and in the abbot or prioress (RB 2:2; 63:13).
Sometimes the "guest" is someone we don't like; St. Benedict
asks us to respect and pray for the person "out of love for Christ"
(RB 4:72). God's incarnate presence is not limited to Jesus of
Nazareth as he lived on earth; God lives on in all people. When
we look at life through the eyes of Benedict, we will see more
than is immediately evident; we can then respond with faith
that God is in this place, this person, this event.

There is no line of demarcation between the sacred and the
profane, between the holy and the material. Everything is holy.[3]
St. Benedict urges the person in charge of the storeroom and supplies (the cellarer) and others who are in charge of material goods
to care with respect as if they are holy objects (RB 31:10). We are
given similar challenges: treat things with care rather than thinking of them as easily disposable and replaceable; respond to
people we are serving with patience, a sense of service, and joy.

St. Benedict also says things are to be handled carefully and
cleaned after being used (RB 32:4). If you break something, you
take responsibility for it (RB 46:1-2). We all know the challenge
of acting responsibly when things belong to everyone and no one
in particular: emptying the water out of the iron, picking up waste
paper from the floor, washing the dirty dishes instead of leaving
them in the sink, and replenishing cooking supplies. St. Benedict
asks that clothing be cared for, and it should fit properly and
match the season (RB 55). Those who have gone on a journey
are to wash their underclothing before returning it to the general
closet (RB 55:13). Because the material world is God's creative
work, it deserves respect and use by responsible stewards.

The world is where we encounter God. Whatever happens in it
can shift our vision, transform our heart, and move us through

dying to fuller life in Christ. St. Benedict shows us how to live so that "in all things God may be glorified" (1 Pet 4:11; RB 47:9). His instructions flow from his focus on Christ, who, as the incarnation of God's love, is God-become-visible. As with Christ, our deepest and most unrelenting desire needs to be for God and to do what we can to enable God's love to permeate the world. As we respond to this basic calling as Christians, our hearts will expand to welcome the persons, things, and events of our daily lives.

Rich with Pennies

When I am tempted to doubt the value of everyday encounters, I often recall Annie Dillard's *Pilgrim at Tinker Creek*. She says, "There are lots of things to see, unwrapped gifts and free surprises. The world is . . . studded and strewn with pennies."[4] Dillard explains that these pennies are the simple, hardly noticeable events in life—events we might disdain and see as unimportant. However, she also points out that we don't get excited by a mere penny nowadays. A friend of mine doesn't pick up pennies anymore. She believes that with the current rate of inflation it's not worth bending over to get it from the ground. She winces when I remind her that Dillard says we need to "cultivate a healthy poverty and simplicity, so that finding a penny will literally make . . . [our] day."[5] Some experiences will remain "pennies." Some will make us rich.

A few years ago I stopped at a local craft store to get a frame for a photo my brother had given me. I found one. It was an exact match of color, and the price was right. But I couldn't tell if my photo would fit in the frame. It had a wide white margin around it—a border I planned to trim according to the size of the frame.

I went to the framing service to get a tape measure. A young woman had placed a shadow box and a couple of tiny baby items on the counter. Among the items was a short, white tape measure. "Perfect!" I thought. I asked her if I could use it to check my photo with the frame.

She held back and said, "It's my baby's."

I felt affronted. Sarcastically I thought: "Maybe she is afraid of getting my germs on the tape."

I caught my irritation and deciding not to leave in such a negative state, I engaged in a few words of conversation. When I commented appreciatively about the items displayed in the shadow box, the woman thanked me and said she wanted advice from a framing consultant about how to attach the items. The clerk took her to the adhesive shelf to point out some tapes that would work. Then she returned and helped me.

The young woman and I met again at the checkout counter. I commented: "I see you found some tape for your project."

"Yes," she said, "but it's so hard."

I must have looked puzzled. She went on to say: "My baby boy died."

Something stabbed my stomach. I told her I was sorry and asked how old he was.

"Five months; he was stillborn."

What could I say? I mumbled, "I'm sorry." Remembering that one of the items for her shadow box was a picture of Christ as the Good Shepherd, I presumed she was a Christian so I added my commitment to pray for her. She thanked me and walked out. And I choked down my tears and left for home.

I found a "penny" when my need for a tape measure or ruler drew me into conversation with the woman. I quickly noticed a deeper poverty—my irritation. The later conversation with the young woman at the checkout counter was an added gift. I gained an understanding of her situation and entered into it emotionally. Humility grounded me as I realized my self-righteousness in judging her reactions when I asked to use her tape measure. I also felt the armor of my defensiveness collapse.

The world is indeed "studded and strewn" with pennies. I'm glad I picked up those I found at the craft store. I left the store a rich woman. Furthermore, I had met Christ who was suffering, and in the midst of the pain I received the healing of compassion even though I was bruised with embarrassment about my hostile thoughts. As I have reflected on the incident, I have grown in hope that my caring encounter brought some consolation to this suffering Christ. I realized, too, that I can bring Christ's healing compassion to people and the rest of creation.

Creation: Manifestation of God

God sings out God's love, magnificence, and extravagance through the created universe. Those who see, hear, touch, smell, and taste well get to notice. They get to marvel. They get to be grateful. Wonders await us: the first violet in spring, the tiny hands and feet of a newborn baby, the ravines on the aged face of an uncle, a cool breeze at the end of a hot day, the odor of manure on a nearby field in spring, a few fluent words spoken by a child who stutters. Such gifts help us come to know by experience that the loving presence of God permeates the universe.

Artists help us notice and appreciate what we often miss. They also encourage us to draw from our memories and imagination. Gerard Manley Hopkins, SJ, spills out his exuberance for all creation:

> The world is charged with the grandeur of God.
>   It will flame out, like shining from shook foil;
>   It gathers to a greatness, like the ooze of oil
> Crushed.[6]

The psalmist reminds us that the world exists as God's creation and self-manifestation. We also receive words for a response when our own might fail us:

> O Lord, how manifold are your works!
>   In wisdom you have made them all;
>   the earth is full of your creatures.
> Yonder is the sea, great and wide,
>   creeping things innumerable are there,
>   living things both small and great. (Ps 104:24-25)

> What are human beings that you are mindful of them,
>   mortals that you care for them?
>
> Yet you have made them a little lower than God,
>   and crowned them with glory and honor. (Ps 8:4-5)
>
> O come, let us sing to the Lord;
>   let us make a joyful noise to the rock of our salvation!
> Let us come into his presence with thanksgiving;
>   let us make a joyful noise to him with songs of praise!
>   (Ps 95:1-2)

A dialogue about the surprises released when ordinary things and people are encountered with a new perspective and awareness opened this reflective expression in my friend Sylvia.

Out of the Ordinary

out of a background of obviousness
in midst of the mundane,
the usual and ordinary of living
a moment, an awakening, an "aha"
perhaps called forth in surprise

in anger, in a giggle of joy,
within depth of despair,
in a splash of beauty
from an unexpected hug, a familiar face
letting you in on a secret intimacy
opening you to a secret intimacy

an opening, an awareness
a glimpse of the Divine
discernment, consciousness,
something never claimed before
but always there . . . or was it

a God-speak moment,
a sacred gift of divine love
revealed in the unique, yet common
in an unpredictable presence
of grace and respondent gratitude.[7]

In the midst of the acclamations of these poets, we realize that sounds, colors, designs, textures, and movements cannot express adequately what our hearts, expanded in wonder and appreciation, want to convey. Wonders are indescribable; they are ineffable. We utter what often seem to be monosyllables, and at times we stand in silence. God is an extravagant giver. As we receive the "pennies" strewn across our path, our pockets will bulge and even spill over.

The Ineffable Inhabits All

Abraham Joshua Heschel states that "the ineffable inhabits the magnificent and the common, the grandiose and the tiny facts of reality alike."[8] Many of us readily admit to the "ineffable" being manifested through the magnificent, the grandiose, and the dramatic events where our attention is grasped and the effects are easily noticed. Even when we acknowledge ordinary events, we are poised to step over them. We are not satisfied with what theologian Peter Fransen describes as God the Father discreetly dropping a hint to his children that he is with them.[9]

Do we really believe and recognize that God's love overflows into all of creation and continues to surround us? Do we trust that the God who became incarnate in Jesus Christ continues to disclose God's self to us? When we come to believe, and as we experience encounters as hints of the presence of our loving God, we will expect and welcome them as extraordinary encounters with ordinary persons, things, places, and events. We anticipate meeting God in any experience. Indeed, we will exclaim with Gerard Manley Hopkins that "The world is charged with the grandeur of God," even in and through the daily bits and pieces of our lives.

Chapter 2

Parables of Awakening

Let us get up then, at long last, for the Scriptures rouse us
when they say: It is high time for us to arise from sleep
(Rom 13:11). Let us open our eyes to the light that comes
from God, and our ears to the voice from heaven that every
day calls out this charge: If you hear his voice today, do
not harden your hearts *(Ps 94 [95]:8).* (RB Prol 8-10)

When We Are Awake

As a young monastic I looked forward to Advent. I anticipated Christ coming in various ways as I waited for his arrival
at Christmas. I didn't know how he would come or what he
would look like, but I expected that something dramatic would
happen. I waited eagerly. I was attentive. I was awake.

By mid-Advent I was disappointed that every day I still
walked in the midst of my usual activities and relationships,
mediocrity and tensions. Through several Advents and other
experiences in my monastic life, I have learned that Christ often
slips into our lives without drama, subtle and unnoticed even
by those who are attentive.

St. Benedict calls for waking up, arising from sleep, and noticing God's action. He realizes that people are drowsy, going
through their daily routine in habits that keep them comfortable and unaware of what is going on within and outside them.
Changes in perceptions, feelings, and actions are not evoked
easily. People are deprived of feelings they could claim as their

birthright, expanded views of the world, and enlarged hearts that open to persons and events that could enrich their lives.

St. Benedict would have enjoyed environmentalist Barry Lopez's description of his wonder when he was surprised as he walked down a sidewalk in New York City:

> . . . a tiny spot of green flashed suddenly from the concrete below. I spotted and squatted for a closer look.
>
> Mother Nature! It was grass! Two blades of grass—bright green against the building's dirty granite—were sprouting from roots sunk in a thin line of black grit. How had they survived the indiscriminate feet of New York pedestrians? How could enough sunlight squeeze through the smog to give life to these little plants? I want to grab someone, anyone, and shout: Look at this! It is wonderful![1]

Lopez is awakened! He sees! Wonder and appreciation push out the edges of his heart. He wants others to see the blades of grass, too. Lopez echoes and exclaims God's words about creation: "And God saw that it was good" (Gen 1:10).

What is the value of such gifts that awaken us and catch our attention? Sometimes, as with Lopez, we experience delight and openness to a reality much bigger than the tiny plants at our feet. At times, they help us turn to God and away from what is self-serving, from what closes and tightens our hearts, and we direct our attention and energy for the good of others. Through such experiences, we are affected personally and God's love is nudged further into the universe.

Recently I became aware of a crying child who had been separated from her mother in a supermarket. I sensed the child's fear. I interrupted my shopping and looked around to see if someone who might be the child's mother was in sight. Eventually a relieved mom and sobbing daughter came together. I saw God again touch the world, including me, with tender love.

Sometimes irritation stirs my drowsiness when I am behind an older sister who is walking down the hall ahead of me. I want to move faster. Then I realize: "Someday I'll be the slow-moving one." My tendency to be efficient and productive is revealed by my fast gait and irritation. I take some deep breaths and relax my shoulders. My pace slows. Unexpectedly I feel compassion for the sister and am glad she can still get around as well as she does.

Stepping out of the Ordinary to Refocus

At times we need to interrupt our everyday routine that absorbs our attention and prevents us from seeing. Birthday celebrations let the celebrant stand out from ordinary life to be honored as special and to be recognized for who she is, what she has done, and how she is valued by her friends and family. A walk in the autumn woods opens the senses and brings back to center the energies that we have strewn in many directions. Time apart with a close friend renews a relationship. Solitude and prayerful reading feed our hearts on the vision and values of Christ. Weddings and funerals, Liturgy of the Hours, and Eucharist bring us together as a community to remember, to be grateful, and to celebrate. We do not walk our faith journey alone. Such practices with others ought to be regular parts of our lives. Stepping out of the usual order of our lives to open to what is beyond our doing and habitual reacting brings awareness. Our lives can then keep on making more of us.[2]

St. Benedict structured practices and events into the life of monastics to help us refocus our attention and purpose. *Lectio divina* (prayerful reading) and Liturgy of the Hours at the hinge points of the day (morning, midday, and evening) open us to possible movements of the Spirit, who might find our attention easier to "catch" when we are quiet and centered. The words of Psalm 89, unabashedly proclaiming that God's love is abundant and enduring, pull me upright in the pew. Readings from the New Testament urge me to feed the hungry, to reconcile relationships, and to open my heart to include all. Rituals open me to transcendence. They help to make more of us—monastics and others who adapt such practices to their lives. We become fuller expressions of God.

In June 2005, my monastic community engaged in a formative ritual when we celebrated the installation of our new prioress. With the gesture of placing our folded hands in hers, all 250 of us ritually expressed our support for her and our obedience to her leadership. As I performed this gesture and watched my monastic sisters do the same, I felt connected to them and to our foremothers who lived before and with us throughout our 150 years in Minnesota. I sensed that we entrusted ourselves again to each other and to monastic life and the mission of our community. We stepped out of the ordinary for a few hours during which our everyday lives were "lifted up" for renewal and recommitment. We then returned changed to our usual activities. Judging from sisters' comments, we became more appreciative of our history and aware that the sacred story of our community continues through us today. We also experienced a calling that will make a difference in how we move into the future together.

Daily Encounters: Parables of God's Love

The dynamics of crises and incidental events in our daily lives follow the pattern of many of the parables, the brief stories Jesus told to depict and evoke the transformation of the world in God's love. Matthew relates that "the kingdom of heaven is like treasure hidden in a field, which someone found and hid; then in his joy he goes and sells all that he has and buys that field" (13:44).

Jesus draws from people's ordinary lives as he spins his parables to make a point. Similarly we write our own parables—in handwriting and in action—using our own and others' experiences. One parable I claim for myself was birthed from an encounter with a salad dressing bottle.

Noon lunch was often a scramble in the house where other students and I lived while doing doctoral studies in Pittsburgh. About eight of us often gathered around the same time before heading off to class. We would take out the makings of sandwiches and salads from the refrigerator. Usually we were in a hurry. Many of us worked until the last minute, grabbed a bite to eat, and dashed out to catch the city bus four blocks away. The bus didn't wait for anyone. We all knew we had to be on it or wait another half hour, which meant we would be rushing into class late. The open seats typically would be in the far back corner of the crowded room, so to come late meant a cumbersome entrance.

One day I automatically slipped into the tenor of the lunch rush. As I grabbed the bottle of salad dressing, it slipped from my hands, landing as a mess of broken glass and red liquid on the floor.

How humiliating! My awkwardness went public. I must have looked very foolish. And I had to use time to clean up the clutter.

While my experience with the salad dressing bottle did not yield a precious pearl, it did turn out to be a parable for me. Philosopher Paul Ricoeur notes that the pattern of many parables includes an encounter, a reversal or change of heart, and a decision to act in accord with what is now valued.[3] As in the parable of the man who found the buried treasure, my encounter stopped me. My hurriedness was interrupted. In the midst of my chagrin, some of my companions pitched in and helped me clean up the debris.

The experience was dramatic enough to keep me thinking about it for several days. Gradually the "buried treasure" opened to greater clarity. I saw myself before the bottle slipped out of my hand. How embarrassing when seen from a later perspective! I realized my tendency to work to the last minute, to be unrealistic about what I could do within a given time, and to forcefully cram my expectations into a small envelope of time. This realization opened possibilities for me to change my attitudes and actions. I could become less driven. I could befriend time rather than relate to it as a competitor. My misfortune gave me another blessing. I surrendered to receiving care and help from those around me. The parable of the man finding the buried treasure became mine as it portrays this sequence: an interruption, then a shift in perception that gives at least one new possibility, and finally a change of heart that aligns a response with what the person values.[4] I claim the incident as a graced moment. "God [and I] saw that it was good" (Gen 1:10b).

But how can such ordinary occurrences as dropping a salad dressing bottle or finding a treasure in a field possibly speak of the kingdom of God? They are so mundane. Where is the drama? Humility will help us trust and see the action of the Spirit in what seems to be subdued tones. We hear a parable and we give another look. Even a slight change for good is valuable. Over time changes will transform us, even though we probably will not notice what is happening. The dropped salad dressing bottle comes to mind often and continues to teach me about gracious living. I am now more aware of when I am being unrealistic about what I can do in the time available. When I catch myself, I gain freedom to choose how I want to be and act. I'd say I've found a pearl in a salad dressing bottle.

Ricoeur points out the ordinariness of the images Jesus uses in the parables:

> [They] are radically profane stories. There are no gods, no demons, no angels, no miracles, no time before time, as in the creation stories, not even founding events as in the Exodus account. Nothing like that, but precisely people like us: Palestinian landlords traveling and renting their fields, stewards and workers, sowers and fishers, fathers and sons; in a word, ordinary people doing ordinary things: selling and buying, letting down a net into the sea, and so on. Here resides the initial paradox: on the one hand, these stories are . . . narratives of normalcy but on the other hand, it is the Kingdom of God that is said to be like this. The paradox is that the *extraordinary* is *like* the *ordinary*.[5]

The topics and episodes Jesus talks about are like those I experience. If they are good enough for him, might I claim them, too? Any event can give me an opportunity for a change of heart that aligns with Christ's, no matter how slight the shift might be. Action in harmony with this change can follow. Every time these dynamics occur, another parable is "written."

Some parables evolve from ecstatic experiences such as a retreat or a landscape scene that moves us beyond our ordinary lives. But they are not usual and we do not remain in them indefinitely. We come down off the proverbial mountaintop and meet the people and tasks of our everyday lives, often hum-drum and disappointing. A crisis pulls us through its own para-bolic action of catching our attention, shifting our perceptions, and calling us to changes in attitude and action. Sometimes I think these dramatic events are the ones that are significant for my life journey. While they certainly can be, we remain grounded in our everyday lives: phone calls, cooking meals, washing dishes, feeding children, and performing the tasks required by our jobs. It seems daily life is a favorite site where the Word of God continues to become flesh.

Life and Healing for All

Each of us serves as a "parable initiator," a provoker of insight as we encounter people around us. Pete, the nine-year-old nephew and godson of Larry, played this role when he gave his testimonial, "Every Moment with Larry," at the time of Larry's college graduation celebration:

> Hi, guys!
> Every moment with Larry is like being with God.
> He is fun, cool and you can't get bored of him.
> It's hard not to see him because he has such a big heart.
> He is the best godfather ever.
> You can't imagine how good he is to me.
> He would help you with anything he could.
> Thanks a bunch, Larry.

It is clear that Larry has formed Pete's perspective, not only of himself as a godfather but also of what is important in life. Each of their encounters served as a "parabolic" interruption. These events helped form Pete's mind and heart and prompted responses such as this testimony to a man with "a big heart." With forthright candor, Pete witnessed to Larry's influence in his life. Pete, in turn, became a parable initiator for Larry, who received an opportunity to recognize his influence on his godson.

What might Larry and Pete teach us about the role of parents in the lives of their children? How can we initiate a parable experience that helps shift the quality of life of someone with whom we live? What can we learn from Jesus, whose life and teachings challenged the status quo, who showed that God's love is inclusive—of people who are poor and of people who are political and cultural outsiders? The biblical image that we are the Body of Christ can shape our perception and actions (1 Cor 6:15a; 12:27). Everyone is part of Christ. Each of us plays a role in the vitality of the whole. Reflecting on and experiencing something of this truth helps us deepen our trust in it and exercise responsibility for the good of all.

Thin Places

Various situations serve as "thin places" where God breaks into our usual, common lives and catches our attention, stirs possibilities of new perceptions and choices, and moves us to action.[6] We wake up. We remain alert for even slight movements of the Spirit. The Irish people recognize that although God is everywhere, there are "spots where this world and the realm of the spirit come close together . . . there are some places like some chords in music that evoke something spiritual in people, as the smell of burning leaves can bring back childhood to many of us, and that some places have more of that power of evocation than others."[7] In such places we are more open than usual to "touch and be touched by God."[8]

Thin places often happen in the midst of daily life. When my schedule is overloaded and makes me tired, I stop and set priorities and allow myself some breathing space between events. A thin place has become palpable. Currently I am struggling to understand why a friend is afflicted with excruciating pain day after day; God does not answer my pleas for relief and I'm challenged to trust anyway. God is pulling me into a thin place. An invitation to participate in a service trip has given me an opportunity to become involved in face-to-face service to those who are homeless. I feel challenges to my fear and resistance to face the dire situations in which some people eke out an existence. I am pushed to say no to the fear that holds me back from giving. In this thin place, challenge awaits me and calls me to make choices that will make more of me as a person in the image of Christ. At the end of the school term a student cites some examples of learning that he gained from the class I taught; I feel lighthearted because I am fostering life, the life of a member of the Body of Christ. All these "thin places" bring me into meeting God and responding with a fuller heart. Sometimes the moments are quite transparent and I am conscious of them. At other times I pass them by or give them only a nodding recognition. God's abundance continues with a constant flow of opportunities. Living mindfully, attentive to what is happening around me and stirring within me, opens me to possibilities to respond with choice.

Knowing the possibilities for meeting God in the everyday, we are more apt to stay awake and to sharpen our recognition skills. We might risk letting ourselves be awakened even more because we know we will be waking up in God's love. As Benedict urges: "*It is high time for us to arise from sleep* (Rom 13:11). Let us open our eyes to the light that comes from God and our ears to the voice from heaven that every day calls out this charge: *If you hear his voice today, do not harden your hearts* (Ps 94 [95]:8)" (RB Prol 8b-10). With hearts that yearn and strain for a personal relationship with God, we are able to trust that we can give ourselves to this God and God's vision for the world.

"Cotton wool of daily life"[9]

Virginia Woolf peered into our daily lives when she wrote that we get fixed in "the cotton wool of daily life." She caught the situations where our routine, ordinary lives often dull us. We do not really see people around us; they have become commonplace. We do not truly hear what family and friends say. We live with unexamined assumptions, drifting through our days without choosing our values, motives, and actions. This dullness becomes hazardous and deadening.

It is difficult to loosen "the cotton wool" from our consciousness. When we do, even if only a little, we are able to move through our encounters with greater openness. However, deep down I resist pulling off the "cotton wool." Sometimes I don't want the responsibility of living consciously.[10] Besides, seeing more clearly most likely will call for uncomfortable changes. I shut out information about people suffering from natural disasters, the controversial actions of our government within and outside the United States, and unjust decisions being made at work. I do not want to feel the pain others are going through or what might threaten me. I do not want to open to the challenge of becoming involved in some type of action.

Even when we are aware and begin a process of changing, we often fall back into our patterns. Czeslaw Milosz' reflection "Beyond My Strength" says it aptly for me: to step back from our usual perspectives and ensuing actions is as difficult for us as it is for a "fly whose leg is stuck in glue."[11] For example, my usual self-righteous comments and blaming nip at the heels of my decision to hold back from judgmental remarks and to instead make comments that are compassionate. In another instance, I am successfully working within a timeline and meeting due dates and then find myself backsliding into procrastination. I feel as though I brace one leg on the glue so I, as the fly, can pull off the other one. I keep sticking to the glue—first one leg and then the other.

Milosz' image pushes each of us to reflect further on ourselves. What is our ordinariness, our routine? What usual ways of seeing and doing keep us stuck? What draws us to want to get off the "sticky glue," our usual perspectives and habits? In what ways do we experience one of our legs sticking to the glue as we try to change? What happens when we try to free a leg? What can help us gain freedom from the glue? The answers to these questions and what we do in response to them will make the difference between freely choosing and being stuck.

Parables, cotton wool, and flies stuck on glue might strike us as unlikely partners and teachers. However, they portray some of the dynamics of awakening. As parables, encounters in everyday life remove some "cotton wool," shift our perspective, and give us opportunities for actions of our choosing. As the "cotton wool" of unquestioning views is peeled away from our eyes and the holding power of routine, "sticky glue," lessens, we take new steps characteristic of a loving heart.

The Parable of the "Walking Madonna"

The postcard brought a few words from a friend who was traveling around England. "I wish you were here to see the wonders we are seeing. Yesterday we visited Salisbury Cathedral. . . ." The personal message slipped from my mind rather quickly, but the "Walking Madonna," a statue pictured on the postcard, lingered for a long time. Dame Elisabeth Frink's six-foot, bronze sculpture stands on the lawn near the cathedral. She is walking with a determined and energetic stride. Her goal is summed up in a few words printed on the postcard: "The woman [is] walking with purposeful compassion as a member of the Community of the Risen Christ to bring love where love is absent."[12]

Initially I could not put into words why the woman caught and held my attention. Was it that her sense of purpose, determination, and courage portray something about my own hopes and how I want to achieve them? Was I fascinated because she embodies one of my favorite passages from St. Benedict when he says that monastics will experience an expanding heart as they run the way of God's commandments with inexpressible delight of love (RB Prol. 49)?[13] Did I instinctively realize that she symbolizes the attitudes, gait, and energy my Benedictine community needs as we live our mission of bringing the good news of Jesus Christ to people today?

During the days after I received the postcard, I noticed times when I felt as confident and energetic as the "Walking Madonna." My inner gait through the day was swift, sometimes running. At other times I felt confused and in conflict. During the unsettled times I found myself asking questions that begged for answers. To what am I running? Is anyone running with me? How do I run when I feel I am trudging, dragging my heels, stumbling, or slogging my way through situations that are bogging me down? How can I run when I am tired, hurting, or doubtful? How can I run with an expanded heart when it is tight, shut down in fear and resentment? As I strive to continue day after day, how can I exercise so my heart expands to give and receive more? How can I move through all the events of the day, whether they be routine, stressful, or delightful, with appropriate timing and a gracious flow on my journey?

These questions were partially answered when another friend gave me her photograph of the "Walking Madonna" that showed a different angle of the statue.[14] I caught sight of a second figure in the background. An elderly woman, supported by a cane, carefully shuffled her way along the sidewalk. I wondered: Which woman is walking with a greater sense of purpose and vigor—the physically strong, striding woman or the vulnerable, shuffling one? How could I measure? Is it important to be able to measure inner vitality and progress on the path to God?

The two women have served as a parable that has continued to open my perceptions and influence my attitudes and choices. They prompted questions about some of my usual standards of judgment. I realized that maybe what's important is that I persevere and keep putting one foot in front of the other rather than being able to see great strides toward my goals. Even a slow pace is movement. Perhaps the emphasis needs to be on purposeful compassion and whatever efforts I give to bring love more fully into my experiences, even when I don't feel I'm doing much or see results. I am courageous even when my fear,

Photograph of Elisabeth Frink's "Walking Madonna" and second woman by Marie Biddle, SJ. Used by permission of Marie Biddle.

discouragement, and fatigue try to tell me I am not. Counter to many societal norms, when I admit my need and ask for help in my work, I am expressing inner strength even when I falter in my asking. Prayer and solitude are fruitful, though they may not produce immediate tangible results in tasks performed. Giving hospitality does not always need to feel easy to be genuine. Inner vitality is marked by my commitment to see and give to Christ in people even when I don't feel generous. Both women in the photo speak to me of walking through my daily experiences with intention, faithfulness, and responsibility for God's purpose, even when I feel fainthearted.

Fifteen years ago the "Walking Madonna" came into my life through a seemingly ordinary event one morning: reading my mail. She caught my attention. I continued to be drawn back to her to ponder what she had to say to me. The message of the woman deepened and expanded later when, through another seemingly ordinary encounter, I met the older woman in the second photograph. Together, the women have provided provocation and inspiration for me personally and for reflection during workshops I have facilitated. I have found that the participants know both these women within themselves: the energetic walker who feels undaunted and effective at times and in other situations the vulnerable and valiant shuffler who steps carefully while relying on her cane for support. I have also discovered that the participants ask the same questions I ask about walking, running, and trudging, about perseverance and exercise, about supports and challenges. We have been drawn together with a sense of our common journey. Over the years the "Walking Madonnas," the younger and the elderly, have become my sisters, and we have walked together. I am grateful they have served as parables for me. I am glad they have helped me find them over and over in myself and in the people I encounter in my daily life. They repeatedly help me to renew my commitment to "bring love where love is absent."

My encounters with the "Walking Madonna" illustrate the ways daily experiences can make a difference for us and for others. We are not able to predict which events will catch our attention or what their influence will be. We cannot control their degree of impact or when it will turn out to be extraordinary. However, some shifts in perspective, inner change, and action are available to us. We need to develop our awareness so more of our daily encounters can become "thin places" where we meet God and respond to the invitations, often only hints, to love in attitude and action. Furthermore, engaging in practices such as prayerful reading and talking with wise people helps develop perspectives for interpreting and responding to experiences for good—our own and others. Hence, our encounters more readily become parables for us, and we can serve as initiators and supporters of parables in the lives of others.

Chapter 3

Hospitality:
Who's Knocking at My Door?

All guests who present themselves are to be welcomed as
Christ, for he himself will say: I was a stranger and you
welcomed me *(Matt 25:35). . . . Christ is to be adored*
[in them] because he is indeed welcomed in them.

(RB 53.1, 7)

Welcome, Mom

I am watching my mother, Margaret, read a novel as she sits
in front of the south window in her apartment. Her arthritic
shoulders soak in warmth from the October sun. I have often
teased her that she is a cat, always finding the sun and basking
in it. I warned her that some day she will start to purr. As I
observe Mom, I recall the years when she wished she had time
to read. But her nine children kept her too busy to allow such
luxury. By nighttime she was too tired to do anything but go to
bed. Later, after Mom had raised us children, cataracts in both
eyes thwarted her hopes for reading. After living with diminished sight for several years, she was given what she considered
a miracle: cataract surgery. She could see again. Books then
became her frequent companions.

As my mind drifts into the past, I see our living room with
a wall full of books: two sets of encyclopedias for those of
school age to use for their research projects, a set of novels by

Louisa May Alcott (all with red covers), and three shelves of miscellaneous books (many with worn covers and some without any) that Mom and Dad had purchased when a nearby country school closed. These books became part of our home, and we took them for granted. Although we seldom read them, except for necessity, we considered them to be members of our family.

I realize now that the books served as symbols of Mom and Dad's valuing of education. They presented many worlds for us to explore: China, plants, Yellowstone National Park, the moon, and New England. They provided reminders that we needed to learn to read so we could get into these worlds. I suspect that the books both soothed and evoked Mom's thirst for education. She carried a painful wound, even as an eighty-year-old woman: the ending of her formal education after her sophomore year in high school. As the oldest girl in the family, she was needed at home to help care for her nine younger siblings. Her education had to wait until later; later never came. The books reminded her of a dream unfulfilled. The books around her also helped Mom support her determination to keep her mind active; they were good friends. Her desire for learning kept her inquisitive and absorbing anything she could discover. She refused to give up being a student, even if she wasn't in school.

The sun has moved. Mom doesn't notice. The novel has drawn her into its plot. And suddenly I realize I have been doing more than watching my mother read a book.

What had I welcomed into my afternoon? What had I seen? Where had Mom, my guest, taken me as she became lost in her novel? I had returned to my childhood home, its books, each child's homework spot at the kitchen table, and Mom reading stories to the preschoolers. I felt compassion for my mother; the ache for going to school accompanied her all her adult life. I admired her resoluteness to be open to new experiences. I felt glad that now Mom could finally indulge herself in reading. I was grateful that Mom and Dad's thirst for learning passed on to my siblings and me. Going to college was a given expectation as I anticipated my future. My dream of becoming a teacher even seeped into play activities. I repeatedly instigated playing school during recess; sitting on the street curb made for an orderly classroom. Often I played the role of the teacher. While I reviewed a bit of my mother's life, I purred with a sense of well-being and gratitude.

As I lingered with my mother while she read her book, I noted that the Holy Spirit slipped into my life, caught my attention, received my welcome, and moved me to say, "Thank you! Thank you!"

I continue to be surprised by the spontaneous and surprising ways God encounters me. Sometimes a stimulus evokes a memory, image, or feeling that breaks through to the surface and asks for a caring response. At times a bodily sensation catches my attention. I feel the stimulation of a breeze, the touch of a friend's hand, or pain in my legs and lungs when exercising. What strikes me and bids for my hospitality often comes through what I am doing: the challenges of a task, the delights of a party, impatience with a store clerk. My usual perception and actions are interrupted by persons and things from my immediate world of home, work and leisure, the broader world of my neighborhood and church, and the national and international communities. Any aspect of my world can intrude and catch my attention. Any person or thing can ask for my welcome and become my guest. Opened eyes and new perspectives become available. Possibilities for an expanded heart await me.

We Are Guests of God, the Arch Host

I appreciate stories of my Reuter and Langenfeld grandparents. Grandma Reuter used to welcome her children as each came home from school and told her about the day's events. Often stories were repeated. Grandma listened to each report of incidents as if it were her first time hearing about them. I marvel at accounts of her patience and generosity. I appreciate the influence of her hospitality to each child. She helped them learn that the world is a good place to be and that they are significant in it. Implicitly, they experienced God's hospitality through her.

Grandpa Langenfeld stayed at our house when he came to town from the farm to serve a couple days of jury duty. I hadn't thought of him doing anything besides farm chores. I learned something of my civic duty through him, even though I would not have used these words at that time. As a citizen in God's world, he also knew he had responsibilities in it, and he performed them. Grandpa and Grandma Langenfeld were the first in their area to get a car—a 1934 Ford Sedan. However, Grandpa was afraid to drive, so Grandma did. Both she and Grandpa became the butt of derogatory comments about who wears the pants in the family (the one who drives) and who is overstepping societal expectations (women don't drive). But Grandma was one who did what needed to be done, and she seized the moment to do it, whether or not people approved. She had developed the wisdom to know she needed a perspective and heart broader than the limiting expectations that society tried to put on her.

I was born into the world of these people. I have their stories and energy in my cells. They taught me to be open to possibilities wherever I am. They educated me well to exercise respect and hospitality for people, including myself. I know, too, that others have given me a tradition in which to form my values and live my life. Two ancestors—Abraham and Sarah, whose stories are many generations old—have made hospitality in even dire situations a quality of life that is foundational.

Abraham greeted and cared for three strangers who came as unexpected visitors to him and Sarah (Gen 18:1-15). Tradition names these guests as representatives of God. Scripture scholar Demetrius Dumm, OSB, opened the text for me to see the hospitality of both Abraham and God. Three visitors approached Abraham, intruding in his activities. They repeated God's promise to give him and Sarah a son. Dumm gets into Abraham's skin and heart and feels his possible reactions. He notes that Abraham could have resented the interruption. He could have been begrudging as he let them come onto his land. However, Abraham had a gift of being ready to look for good in unexpected and unplanned events.[1] Dumm notes: "Abraham is no reluctant or merely dutiful host. He hastens to prepare a feast for his guests, the dimensions of which are almost as extravagant as the promises of God had been."[2]

God, as the three visitors, received generous hospitality from Abraham and Sarah. The menu was fantastic. The food was prepared with microwave speed. A sumptuous meal was served. Indeed, not only was Abraham open to surprises but he also moved into extravagant action. He reflected God's flair for hospitality.

But where was God's hospitality? God offered the hospitality of a renewed promise of a son to Abraham and Sarah. They were given a surprise: the pledge would be fulfilled soon. In light of their advanced age, these assurances certainly must have been challenging to accept. Abraham could easily have been cynical at yet another promise that probably would not be fulfilled. In his reflection on the promise and its renewals, Dumm opens the promise so we can see that it extends beyond Abraham and Sarah.[3] Nations, as well as Abraham and Sarah, will be blessed. God's hospitality is so expansive that it includes all people, then and through all time. God's hospitality is bighearted. It is particular and personal. It welcomes and cares for all people, all creation. God bids us to do likewise.

And so does St. Benedict. He asks monks to greet guests as if they are Christ (RB 53.1). He even goes so far as to say that this type of hospitality is a way of adoring Christ: "Christ is to be adored because he is indeed welcomed in them" (RB 53.7). When the guest is amiable, upbeat, aligned with my values, and free of irritating mannerisms, I find this admonition easy to follow. When people lack these qualities, I am pushed to hang on to Benedict's urging, sometimes by my fingernails, so that I respond with respect, care, and compassion. It is challenging to recognize this Christ. I want a different Christ to meet. However, my faith that Christ lives somewhere in the person and events helps me say yes with as much energy as I can muster. My heart opens enough so I can at least inwardly utter, "I believe. I am trying to be open to you with respect. I bring you God's hospitality."

I am glad that Abraham, Sarah, St. Benedict, and other foremothers and fathers have flourished as part of my family tree. They have served as bearers of the hospitality of God, the arch host. They give me deep roots to support my life and branches to reach out to others. However, I am even more grateful for the originator of hospitality, God the Creator.

God created human beings and welcomed them into creation, particularly into a special garden (Gen 1). Psalms 24 and 8 remind me that God is the creator of the earth and the entire universe. The world belongs to God. In this world God is our host.

> The earth is the Lord's and all that is in it,
>   the world, and those who live in it;
> for he founded it on the seas,
>   and established it on the rivers. (Ps 24:1-2)
>
> O Lord, our Sovereign,
>   how majestic is your name in all the earth!
>
> You have set your glory above the heavens. . . .
>
> When I look at your heavens, the work of your fingers,
>   the moon and the stars that you have established;
> what are humans beings that you are mindful of them,
>   mortals that you care for them? (Ps 8:1, 2a, 3-4)

My hospitality takes on a transforming dynamic when I am aware that God is the arch host who has already made room for us, who honors and appreciates us, and who continues to offer hospitality to us and all creation. Through attentiveness to events in my daily life, I grow in the realization that I am a recipient of God's hospitality. I am God's guest.[4] When I recall this fundamental truth, it radically affects how I live. My vocation is to live in the image of this God, the arch host. Furthermore, I have been given much, and out of the gifts given to me I am called to share my time, skills, things, and presence with others. This responsibility calls me to let go of the arrogance that says, "This is mine," an attitude that fails to recognize my interdependence with others. I must be here for others. I, as well as others, am charged with the responsibility to care for this gift of creation. I am called to give hospitality event by event.

The God We Meet

I keep being reminded that the God I meet is God's choice. I do what I can to be open to the revelations of God, but I cannot control when or in what form God will say, "Here I am." I know God to be relentless in being God and not subject to revealing or acting as I want. Furthermore, when I think I have gotten to know God, I discover that God differs from the one I envisioned and is beyond my imagining. I am continually invited to discover that God as God appears to me in each situation. I have been challenged repeatedly to believe that whatever face of God is revealed, I am being given an opportunity to be touched and moved, and to walk forward with an expanded heart.

I met the magnificent God on an airplane flight to Seattle a few years ago. As we were dropping altitude prior to landing, Mount Rainier suddenly loomed into view outside my window. We were flying very close to and parallel with this "goddess." She was showing off her grandeur. She reigned over the terrain below. I became oblivious of everything around me. As we landed, I realized that an ordinary flight suddenly had brought me a few moments of ecstasy.

A few years later I flew to Seattle again. I made sure I sat on the side of the plane from which I had the best chance to see Mount Rainier as we flew near our destination. Alas, this time the goddess was covered with clouds. I strained to see through them; I desperately wanted to push the clouds aside so the mountain could emerge. Disappointment and frustration landed with me. Something told me that I had met the elusive God who surely stood in majesty but who would not obey my demand to be seen.

Recently the God of peace and I encountered each other during *lectio divina,* the prayerful reading I try to do each day. I had read Jesus' instructions to his disciples to pray for peace if it is absent and that it will return if it is missing from where it had been (Matt 10:13). Usually when I read such directives, I quickly move to reviewing situations in my life and my world that are troubled and not at peace. And of course, my pragmatic self wants to do something about it. This day I "got it"—a new perspective: as important as my action might be, making peace is not all about my doing; I am invited to pray for peace to return to where it was or could be before I act. God is the initiator, not I. I am allowed to participate. Again I heard St. Benedict, whose voice seemed to come from over my shoulder, remind me that whenever I begin a good work, I must pray that God will bring it to completion (RB Prol 4).

As I opened space within myself to receive this insight and to shift my energy, I also heard the invitation to look around me and notice where God's hospitality already was bringing peace: the airing of a conflict between friends so wounds could heal, people in recently flooded areas finding solace as others from throughout the region came to help sandbag dikes and shores, and Tutsis and Hutus in Rwanda moving from seeing and calling themselves by their former tribal names that divided them to becoming known to themselves and the outside world as Rwandans. This review of people being blessed with peace helped me trust that, truly, God's care goes before me. This realization moved me to say thanks before saying please in my prayers for people needing peace.

A few years ago I met the God of compassion and gentle surprises of hospitality as I lived for a month without being able to put any weight on my left foot because of a broken metatarsal bone. People often pushed the elevator button for me as I drew near on my motorized cart. Sisters offered to carry my tray at meals. One of the older sisters slipped into my room several times a day and asked if I needed anything. Often my answer was yes: a glass of water, a piece of paper picked up off the floor, a message delivered to someone, an apple brought from the refrigerator. There was no repaying this hospitality. All I could do was to receive it with welcome and with gratitude.

At any time, God welcomes us and comes to be welcomed. I have often asked, "Who is this God?" Answers vary. Some of us have discovered that God is a God of magnificence, transcendence, and mystery who defies our understanding. At times God is elusive, as in a fog, and we wonder where God is; sometimes we question whether God knows and cares about us. At times the God of compassion knocks at my door as a friend who listens to me and accepts me as I struggle to put into words some of my doubts and fears. At other times God is one with whom I wrestle or on whom I depend for help, especially when I am in crisis. We meet the God of surprises in a family member who resolves a conflict in a way we didn't expect. God as disturbing is made known when we are confronted with our own narrow-mindedness and violence; our ideal self-image falters. In the quiet of prayer we might meet the God of intimacy, the God within. The same silence might be an experience of God's absence as we agonize in our need for direction and reassurance of God's presence and care.

As we become more aware of our guest list that notes some of God's appearances and visits with us, we are enabled to grow in trust that God is in the process of keeping the promise made through Christ: "I am with you always, to the end of the age" (Matt 28:20b), a promise that is being fulfilled day by day, event by event.

Dusting: An Opportunity to Caress

For some people, the doors of welcome are often closed to routine and repeated household tasks such as cleaning and cooking. Dusting certainly stands out for me as one of these unwanted guests. But recently Gunilla Norris' poem "Dusting" helped me open my hand of welcome to this task.

> Time to dust again
> Time to caress my house,
> to stroke all its surfaces.
> I want to think of it as a kind of lovemaking
> . . . the chance to appreciate by touch
> what I live with and cherish.
>
> The rags come out—old soft pajama legs,
> torn undershirts, frayed towels.
> They are still of use.
> It is precisely because they have exhausted
> their original use that they have come
> to this honorable task.
>
> Rag in hand, I feel along each piece
> of furniture I live with, and luster returns
> to the old sideboard, to the chair legs
> and the lamp stands. It is as if by touch
> they are revealed and restored to themselves.
> Strange that in the dumbness of inanimate things
> one can feel so much silent response.
> What then of us animate creatures?[5]

When I read this part of the poem to my friend Anne, her response opened further the door of my hospitality to this ordinary domestic activity. She gave me a list of reasons why she likes to dust. She enjoys dusting furniture and the pegs of the railing on the stairs. She likes to feel the texture of the wood and to smell the lemon-scented dusting oil. Anne finds that dusting gives her head a rest from thinking about her classes, research, and the activities she is planning. She welcomes and appreciates that dusting can give her a sense of accomplishment. She has something to show for her work.

Even with Anne's embracing responses, I was still tempted to blurt out to both her and Norris: "You've got to be kidding!"

I question: How can dusting be, as the poem states, like love-making? Like caressing and stroking? Surfaces and textures appreciated and respected? Helping to reveal and restore luster? It would take some convincing for me to invest time and energy in such a mundane activity with the enthusiasm these friends give it.

However, the poet brings me back to reconsider the ordinary actions of my day and consider another point of view. It usually doesn't take much reflecting to observe that there is more to daily experiences than what I notice on first glance. When I offer hospitality to such daily tasks, they gift me with something more than functioning. My senses become active: I smell, taste, hear, touch, and see. Appreciation, enjoyment, and graciousness touch the tasks I otherwise might just want to be completed so I can move on to another project. In the midst of a fast-paced life that tends to keep my body taut and my brain functioning at full capacity, household tasks slow me down and bring me into my body and put my feet on the ground. I then am able to "appreciate" and "cherish."

The last section of Norris's poem reflects on dusting as an analogy. She moves from the silent responsiveness of inanimate things as they are "revealed" and "restored to themselves" to the effects of caring for human beings.

> We are so many-surfaced: bumpy, smooth,
> prickly, rough, silky, hairy, spiny, soft, scaly,
> furry, feathery, sharp, and on and on.
> And don't we all want to be stroked in some way
> . . . to be restored to ourselves by touch
> as much as by sight or smell or sound.

Whenever I read this section of the poem, a dam of images breaks open. A variety of people, things, and events cascades over my internal screen: Jude, the student who struggles to connect religion and science; Danny, whose exuberance about caring for the land and the production of healthy food motivates him to work for an organic community garden; Petra, who can be counted on to shift any conversation to her own experiences and interests so she becomes the center of attention; myself when I struggle with believing that I am accepted by people around me even though I am crabby and not as productive as I think I should be; Jesus, whose heart was large and pushed him to provide bread and fish for the crowd (Matt 14:13-21; Mark 6:34-44; Luke 9:10-17; John 6:1-13); Jairus, who asks Jesus to heal his daughter who is near death (Luke 8:40-42, 49-56); Georgia, who is angry at God because her mom was not healed of cancer; Justin, who recently rediscovered his joy in climbing trees and who now scales his favorite tree and practices centering prayer in a fork in the top branches. "Many-surfaced" people fill the metaphorical screen of any of our days with varying degrees of impact. Furthermore, each person is "many-surfaced," with numerous roles, varying moods, values, and perspectives. We meet different faces of each other. We stroke each other as we meet in our daily encounters. We meet the God who chooses to reveal God's self in each and who asks for our welcome and caring responses.

Norris points out that she will reveal and restore the luster of the object as she dusts it. She challenges me to think further about the metaphor. All of us are given opportunities to stroke each other and in so doing we will both "luster" and "be lustered." This highlighting of our texture and inner form will probably occur in events as seemingly insignificant as dusting furniture and pegs on a railing. Norris graces all of us with the reminder that our receiving and giving will enable us to receive and give God's "inward touch." We meet God and God's ways of coming into our midst. A few caring strokes bring God's love into the world.

> I want to be a lover of surfaces all day today.
> Let this be the prayer:
> that my hands not be ashamed
> to give and to receive a passionate exchange
> . . . to luster and to be lustered . . .
> And so come to feel Your inward touch.

I've welcomed Norris and Anne into my prayer as I have reflected on this poem. They are valuable friends to visit periodically. I usually discover, as we linger with each other and move into saying "so long" until our next visit, that I'm holding a metaphorical dust cloth in my hands. And it smells of lemon.

Hospitality to the Unwanted Guest of Pain

I wanted to go. I didn't want to go. I had to go. Immaculée Ilibagiza would be speaking in Minneapolis, an hour away. I didn't want to hear her descriptions of the horrors that occurred during the genocide in Rwanda several years ago. I resisted going into the experience with Ilibagiza, who had been hidden in a small bathroom with seven other women for three months, her suffocating conditions, her panic when she heard the enemy tribesmen outside the door of their hiding place with machetes in hand, and her hunger. In the midst of her suffering Ilibagiza struggled with God, who sometimes seemed to have abandoned her and who, at other times, felt intimately close, keeping alive in her heart her desperate need for God's help.

I'd much rather look at the pain through the healing that has occurred in Rwanda. The documentary *Rwanda Rising* brings me into the cheering section as the country's renewal is based on reconciliation, wise leadership, especially by people willing to return to Rwanda to help it rebuild, creative plans for economic development, and an enlightened new government.[6] In truth, I admit that I want the fruits without all the labors of ground breaking and gardening. I want the resurrection without suffering and death that makes it possible. Before I lost my courage, I arranged for a ticket for admission to Ilibagiza presentation.

I know that people in various parts of the world suffer from desecrating and violent events. But to let myself feel the victim's terror in the face of life-threatening and excruciatingly painful perils is too much for my psyche and heart. I cannot imagine living with the constant threat of bombing and devastating suicides in Iraq. My imagination shuts down when I draw near to Anne Frank's experience of being a Jew-in-hiding in the early 1940s. I don't want to feel the hopelessness and vulnerability of people, especially children, who are homeless or on the verge of losing their homes. I cover my ears so I won't hear the answer to the question: what is the experience of an undocumented immigrant in the United States? Along with resisting feeling the pain of others, I also unconsciously block my anger at the political and economic drives that are resulting in much of the devastation throughout the world. I sense that to let it loose could be overwhelming. My heart is not large enough to let in the pain.

The invitation to know the suffering Christ comes as a challenge to my openness to receive all guests. I will be drawn into the anguish. I will be required to allow space within me and to respond to situations of extreme suffering. I then will need to face, in ways I have not done before, that we all are the Body of Christ and that the suffering of others is mine. And so I must know something of it at least within my imagination, emotions, and actions. Otherwise I am like a detached limb that is not connected to the whole. I am lacking the full vitality that comes from both pleasant and painful experiences. I cannot act on behalf of others as fully as I might. Many calls for hospitality seem to come as long-distance nudging or commands. They often are outside my experience and literally from the other side of the world. However, seen and heard from the perspective of my participation in the Body of Christ, they no longer come as long-distance calls. They come through the media as an ordinary part of my day. They come from people around me. They come from members of Christ. They come from me as part of the Body of Christ.

Hospitality to Time

Time in our Western world is begging for hospitality. I often picture time cowering under the terms we use when referring to it. We *mark it;* we *spend it;* we *kill it.* We feel time *slipping away* from us and *deadlines* that hassle us. In some events we try to *beat the clock.* We *run out of time.* On some occasions we have *time on our hands* and we feel we are *wasting it.* We measure time; it's a *long* or *short* time. It *comes and goes.* We are *on time;* we *have time* or *we don't have it.*[7]

I have observed over the years that this language both expresses and forms our attitudes toward time and our relationship with it. Many of these attitudes, which in turn affect our actions, are counter to the scriptural interpretation of time as holy. Even referring to time as "it" expresses the perspective that it is an object and that it can be controlled and manipulated.

I have tried to modify my language to be more respectful of time but find that English does not offer many alternatives to our usual expressions. Instead our words reveal our adversarial and competitive stance toward time. Our focus on time as a scarce commodity and on accomplishing under *deadlines* that often are killing shows that we are seeing ourselves as its owner. As supposed owners we often hoard time or expect it to produce all we want. Our sense of worth is also challenged when our performance is not as productive as we would like it to be. Thus our adequacy and significance are in question. I repeatedly feel challenged to align my perspective of time, and hence my responses, with God's vision: that all events express in some way God's creative love and that all events invite me to respond in love.

I have found the distinction between *kairos* time and *chronos* time helpful. *Kairos* time is concerned with the now-quality of an event and its goodness without being measured by productivity. *Chronos* time views time as linear and as moving from one event to another. Often we expect it to be productive. Both experiences of time call for integration into our lives. It is not a matter of either/or. What we accomplish is important for the sake of ourselves and others. However, *how* we are present in a situation is at least as important as *what* we are doing. Here I recall a situation that showed me *kairos* time in action.

One day I helped Sister Sarah unrack cleaned dishes. I enjoy this job. I work fast. I feel accomplishment. I appreciate the clean dishes. As we were unracking, I noticed that Sarah's pace was much different from mine. She removed two plates at a time from the rack, one plate in each hand. I could grab four. She slowly and carefully put them on the plate cart. My rate was two or three times faster than hers. I began to wonder how long it would take us to unrack if we went at her pace. This thought disintegrated when St. Benedict's phrase about caring for the things of the monastery slipped in to convict me: "regard all utensils and goods of the monastery as sacred vessels of the altar" (RB 31.10). So, whose way of unracking was better? I heard the answer from St. Benedict.

St. Benedict offers other supports to help monastics to live *kairos* time. He gives many guides for reverence in daily life. We return to his basic urging: Guests are to be welcomed as Christ (RB 53.1). Extending the interpretation of who our guests are, other members of the monastery, ourselves, various other creatures, and events call for respect. Christ is available to meet us in any of these. Utensils are to be kept clean and in repair (RB 32; 35). The cellarer is mandated to care for the storeroom and its contents as well as care for the people who request supplies. St. Benedict directs him to respond always with an encouraging word (RB 31). The oratory and dormitory are to be respected for their purpose; thus they are to be quiet areas so monks can hear the reading and can sleep without disturbance (RB 22; 38). Readers are to be effective so they can edify their hearers rather than irritating them with errors and ill-prepared reading (RB 38). Scratching off the surface of these practical guides, we find St. Benedict's grounding in the Christian perspective: time is holy; we can meet Christ in any situation. Furthermore, we are more than idealistic spirits, so we need to live with our feet on the ground of daily life and with practical supports. We participate in God's creative action in the world; we are called to bring life-supporting qualities to what we do. St. Benedict knew about *kairos* time. He offers guidance to live it as we engage in our daily tasks. His instructions about how to live are available to all of us. Can we risk believing that they make sense when productivity is woven into our identity as persons and as a society?

Rabbi Zalman Schachter also knows about *kairos* time. He notes that joy awaits us through our attention and respect for daily encounters: "There is a disease rampant—a chronic, low-grade depression that never knows how to smack its lips and say 'It is good to be alive!'"[8] I suspect that many of us are caught in the disease but wouldn't give it Schachter's diagnosis. I also conjecture that many of us need to learn various ways to smack our lips.

Since reading Schachter's disease alert, I have asked myself periodically, "What have I smacked my lips about today? Have I really seen, smelled, felt, touched, and tasted the gifts God gave me?" When *chronos* time marks my day, I can usually come up with a list of happenings that help me say, "It was a good day! It is good to be alive." Checking off items on my "to do" list makes it a good day at times.[9] However, this criterion soon wears thin. It is not enough. A "good day" needs to ooze out, at least on the edges, qualities such as gratitude, befriending, presence, respect, perseverance, and service—for others and for myself.

A Blessing, Please

St. Benedict says that when meeting guests the monk is to greet them humbly and to ask for a blessing (RB 53.24). But surely not all guests—persons, things, events—can give a blessing, something for my and others' good. Some are repulsive. Some are too insignificant to make much difference. I sense some will bring pain. Herein lies a challenge for me to face my biases. When am I selective and prejudiced about the source of my blessings? When do I ask, "What blessing can this person, this encounter possibly give me?" Certainly I deserve better. Surely Christ would not come in such inconsequential and even contemptuous ways—for me, for our world. Do I have to believe that disagreeable and even unethical situations can bring blessings? And shouldn't blessings be noticeable and feel pleasant? St. Benedict tells me to receive the guest in all situations, implying that I am to expect a blessing from all of them. I'd rather ignore his urging.

As I think about these reactions, I sense a sneer in my heart, and blessings are slipping away. These reactions that discard possibilities call for discipline so they don't deprive me as well as others of blessings. Attention to whatever blessings might be given helps release their effects. Furthermore, my role is to stand humbly and let God, our host and host of the universe, decide what blessings will be given. Then I will be true to my human calling that requires me to be a receiver as well as a giver. As I receive, I am blessed. As I receive, I mediate God's blessings to others. I bear God's hospitality to the world. I will be a blessing.

Chapter 4

Obedience:
We Listen, Discern, and Respond

*Listen carefully, my son [my daughter], to the master's
instructions, and attend to them with the ear of your heart.
This is advice from a father who loves you; welcome it, and
faithfully put it into practice. (RB Prol 1)*

Cheers for Ryan

Even with his mother's urging, Ryan had been resisting reading his library books. One day he and his mom chatted with the clerk at the checkout counter at the local grocery store. The clerk complained to Ryan how dismayed she was that her grandchildren don't do much reading. She then said to him: "I'm sure you read a lot when you get home from school."

When they were out of earshot of the clerk, Ryan turned to his mother and said, "Mom, I think that was God talking to me—giving me a message about reading. When I get home I'll start reading the book on Hawaii you checked out of the library for me." Under her breath, his mother whispered, "Thank God!"

The situation was just right for the Spirit to intervene. Ryan's resistance to reading and his mother's prodding came together with a concerned grandparent's comments. How surprised Grandma would have been if she had known that her statement of concern and her assumption about Ryan, though inaccurate, made such a difference. For Ryan the message could not have been more direct. He didn't duck its challenge. Who could have anticipated such an important conversion experience to occur during a routine shopping trip?

St. Benedict would have cheered for nine-year-old Ryan as he caught the challenge and resolved to act on it. Benedict's first word of his Rule is "Listen." While intended for monks, his instruction can serve all who choose to walk their life journey consciously. Basic to his urging is the context for the listening: We listen to God who speaks to us and who does so most frequently through incidents of our daily lives. God speaks; we are to listen. Thus we need to open ourselves to the possibilities that become available through interruptions rather than give them only nodding attention, much as a parent does to pacify a child when she is busy or not really interested in what is being said.

Listen with the Ear of Your Heart

"Listen carefully . . . attend . . . with the ear of your heart . . . and faithfully put it into practice" (RB Prol 1). Benedict's metaphor calls us to listen from within, regardless of what is occurring. Readiness to hear, humility, and reverence are essential friends of listening. Listening draws from our intuitions and hunches, memories and reflections as well as what we readily hear in an encounter. At times insights and shifts occur on the spur of the moment, and we move on. Sometimes it is important to wait and be with the experience for a while to learn what comes together or evolves. Over time, implications and interpretations that reveal more messages and meaning can emerge.

As I listen, I might talk with someone who serves as a companion who listens with me. Two people listening to the Spirit speaking through a situation often hear better than one can. Every situation can be seen from more than one viewpoint. My companion may help diminish the power of emotional blocks that are hindering me from the necessary freedom and courage to listen, discern, and respond to what seems to be communicated to or asked of me. Hence, Benedict makes it imperative that listening by the abbot, deans, and individual monastics be done within the context of community. Furthermore, he would say listening is essential for all who want their lives to be directed by God. Benedict realizes that the members of the community can give each other support for their personal journeys. They also serve each other as they listen together in discerning and carrying out their decisions.

Listening Brings Gifts

To what and to whom do we listen? How do we make appropriate responses? What are some positive fruits of such listening and responding?

While the answers to these questions vary, no person, place, thing, or event escapes the realm of possibility for meeting God and for receiving invitations to listen and respond. They step into our lives spontaneously, and they often slip out quickly while leaving us with at least a slight shift in perspective. A table conversation becomes hilarious; I feel lighthearted and grateful. My concern for human rights pushes me to attend a city council meeting and express my opinion about an upcoming decision. The thought of a friend surfaces; I surprise her with a phone call; both of us are glad, and our connection with each other is refreshed.

What do we listen for? How do we listen? While there are no formulas to make listening easy and fool proof, our human and Christian calling gives us our mission that asks for our focus and efforts. We were created to love. Responding affirmatively to this call enables God's love to become embodied in our world today. Love is transforming; our loving brings God's love into the here and now. So we return to the question: what do we listen for? And we receive a gospel answer: listen for invitations to love with its many expressions such as courage, patience, delight, compassion, standing for the truth in what we see, friendship, and care of creation.

Essayist Scott Russell Sanders illustrates both the type of event that can catch our attention and the realizations we might gain through reflection on an experience. While concentrating on reading a book in the hubbub of an airport, he was interrupted. He writes of his attention being caught by a "piercing fragrance":[1]

> Looking up, I saw a woman sitting perhaps twenty feet away, slowly peeling an orange. Sunlight pooled in her lap, illuminating the deliberate movement of her hands. When she had stripped away the last curls of rind, the plump orange lay in her palm like an egg. It looked so vibrant, so potent, it might have been the egg from which the whole universe hatched. Then the woman broke it apart, slid one section into her mouth, closed her eyes, and chewed. After a minute or so, she ate another section, then a third, and so on until she had finished. As I watched her eat, I felt as nourished by that orange as by any food I had ever swallowed. The tang and smell and juicy abundance of the fruit filled me to overflowing.

Sanders was stopped. He was not expecting the encounter. He had come prepared with a book to occupy his time while he waited for his plane. I surmise that the book was feeding into a current writing project, class, or lecture. Reading while waiting would use his time purposefully. Meeting the woman and relishing her enjoyment of the orange changed everything. Delight carried Sanders out of himself. For a few minutes time became timeless. For a few minutes he was not concerned about doing anything productive. Just being present in the sensual ecstasy was enough.

Sanders lingered with the experience. Through reflection his world opened to let in the characters and the action of the scene. He recalled that he readily accepted these entrancing occurrences when he was a child. They were usual and to be expected. Now as an adult, he said, they are fleeting and rare. And yet such experiences of "oneness . . . [are] life's deepest truth." Sanders pointed out that they overcome us with awe and shape our lives. They turn us to the source of our lives, slowly "realigning each cell" in the process of turning. Sanders also realized that in this encounter he was given a sense of a being or power beyond him.

He recognized that the experience was a gift; he could not have predicted or structured it. Sanders acknowledged another gift: the renewal of his commitment to be "present, attentive, open" in his daily life. In this stance his senses were opened to receive whatever blessings become available.

A woman and an orange in an airport along with an attentive and responsive observer merged to create an unexpected sensual blessing. To use Benedict's words, Sanders listened with the ear of his heart to what was going on outside and within himself, at the time of the encounter and through later reflection (RB Prol 1). A seemingly ordinary action, a woman eating an orange, became extraordinary. Sanders returned to waiting for his plane. He was as he had been. Yet he was not the same. He noted of himself: his "inner ruckus" yielded "to stillness and . . . [he was] overcome by awe."

Our Bodies Call Us to Listen

A significant way God reveals care and direction is through our physical being. Twitches in our stomach, hearing our sharp words to a colleague, sweaty palms, feeling lighthearted and energetic, and smelling fresh bread can tell us something. When we are tuned in to our bodily sensations we gain an opportunity to step back and learn what is going on within and outside ourselves. Barbara Myerhoff demonstrated the dynamics of such an experience when she visited survivors of the Holocaust who were living in a center for elderly Jewish people in California. What began as a seemingly insignificant reaction prompted an opening to new and profound insights.

One day Myerhoff joined some residents for lunch. She noticed that they "seemed more contentious than usual. There was endless hassling about the food. People at the tables farthest from the kitchen clamored loudly because they would be served last. Jake didn't like the dessert and tried to sell it to his tablemates. Sam stuffed all the rolls he could reach into his pocket."[2] Myerhoff became irritated:

> My irritation grew as the bowls of oranges and apples were
> passed at the end of the meal. At our table the fruit was snatched
> up immediately, leaving only three bruised apples. Two women
> elbowed each other for the best ones, then looked at me some-
> what sheepishly, noticing that I would be left with the bruised
> apple. I said I didn't mind, and took it with me to eat on the
> way home. But it was completely rotten inside and even though
> I was hungry, I had to throw it away.[3]

Words, gestures, facial expressions, and tangible tension were
evident; Myerhoff could not ignore them. Her physical and
emotional reactions told her something was awry. Her irritation
nudged her to take a second look at the situation involving the
residents and herself. When she did, she discovered that there was
a deeper issue pushing to the fore through the people around the
table. They lived with a history of war and starvation that colored
their present perception and behavior. Rolls, dessert, oranges, and
apples loomed large in the foreground of their meal. Myerhoff
states:

> The selfish women at my table for lunch were themselves too
> bruised to graciously accept a damaged piece of fruit. . . . These
> people themselves were too much like rotten, unwanted fruit.
> Their struggle for the better apples was a small way of repudiat-
> ing their own condition. . . .

> The bruised apple often served as a mnemonic for me, reminding
> me that however vital and joyous and angry the Center people
> were, however adept at asserting their independence, disguising
> their hurts, protecting their pride, they were deeply injured by
> their situation. Without this clear realization, their actions were
> unintelligible.[4]

The gift of reflection! Myerhoff's reflection helped her replace
impatience and intolerance with understanding and compassion. What was happening at the table was more than met the
eye at first glance. The residents were human beings who were
hurting. What Myerhoff saw was only a symptom of a deep
pain that exhibited itself in contention. Furthermore, she real-

ized that the desirable fruit might salve their wounds and ease their pain, at least temporarily. She could no longer disregard these people as cantankerous and annoying. Her inner listening enabled the people to be more than what her first perception could detect.

By giving attention to her feelings, Myerhoff also met herself: the influence of her own hunger, expectations, emotions, and imagination that interacted with the dynamics going on around her, and her perspective as an anthropologist. After sorting out what was going on within herself, she became free enough to accept herself as an emotional human being who experiences a range of feelings, including those we would rather not admit to ourselves. Even as a professional anthropologist, she is susceptible to becoming impatient with people without thinking about their circumstances. She realized that her professional training had equipped her with skills to explore what is going on below the surface that could cause reactions such as emotional upheavals, questions, and impulsive judgments. Myerhoff's experience illustrates how our feelings, hunches, physical sensations, and memories can lead us to give attention to what is at hand and to choose the responses we will make.

Memories and Images Come Forward

Stimulation through our senses calls forth memories, which in turn offer us opportunities for inner and outer shifts. One day I was in a large department store. I became aware of a man's voice behind me. It's my Grandpa Langenfeld! But it can't be; he died twenty years ago. No, it wasn't Grandpa, but the voice so characteristic of him brought him close. I was so enthralled that for ten minutes I followed the man, elderly as was my grandfather, around the store and lingered nearby when he'd stop to look at some merchandise or talk with someone. The past, with some of its stories and characters, became present. After we parted company, I moved lightheartedly and heard Grandpa for hours afterward. Memories of Grandpa walked with me: the crisp dollar bill that each grandchild received as a Christmas gift, Grandpa and my uncles playing poker while the women sat in the living room chatting about family happenings, the pungent smell of his pipe, his endless table prayers as the rest of us waited, more focused on Grandma's hamburgers and mashed potatoes than on Grandpa's Our Fathers and Hail Marys. What a transforming intrusion into my day! Gratitude, connection with my tribe of foremothers and fathers and cousins, joy, and dedication to make family happen marked the event and enlarged my heart.

When we draw near to the feast of Christmas we remember past celebrations. We see people; we feel the sense of the holiday environment; we hear people's voices, Christmas music, and children's merriment. We smell and taste favorite foods. The past returns through our memory and imagination. If the earlier events were happy, we probably will be relaxed and nostalgic and moved into joyful anticipation for the Christmas we are about to celebrate. We might be flooded with gratitude. If Christmas was often a time of discord or marks the time a family walked through the death of a loved one, the day could easily evoke somberness and dread. At such times we receive challenges such as listening within ourselves, to others, to our tone of voice, and to what we are saying. Coming through the discomfort could well be a call to take steps to reconcile with and forgive persons who have hurt us. It could be an invitation to ponder and treasure the loved person who has died or to seek help to move beyond the disruptive pain in our hearts.

Yaffa Eliach, a key initiator of the "Tower of Life" at the Holocaust Museum in Washington DC, described an incident of memory that illustrates some of its dynamics and possibilities for a healing of heart through remembering.[5] As an adult Eliach returned to her destroyed village where many Jews had been killed. She visited the woman who was instrumental in saving her life when she was a young child. When Eliach met her protector, she immediately recalled the smell of the woman's shawl that was used to cover her as she carried her from one building to another. Scenes of moments that her life was threatened inundated her. For a few minutes she returned to being a young child, terrified for her safety. In the midst of Eliach's remembered fear, she was overwhelmed with gratitude for the woman who risked her life on her behalf. Terror and gratitude met each other. The terror diminished as gratitude became her new protective shawl.

A Word Stops Us; We Hear and See

Several years ago as I listened to the gospel story from Luke 8:40-56, I was struck by the interruption Jesus experienced on his way to heal the twelve-year-old daughter of the leader of the synagogue. As Jesus went to heal Jairus' daughter, a woman in the crowd who was suffering from hemorrhage touched the hem of his garment. I had heard and read the passage many times, but this time some new details caught my attention. Jesus was on his way to attend to a child; this service was his work. But he was stopped along the way by someone in need; healing the woman then became his work.

I realized that many times I complain, saying, "I keep getting interrupted and can't get my work done." This episode in Jesus' life led me to reflect on my attitudes and my narrow vision of what my "work" is. I couldn't squirm out of what I realized through Jesus' response to the woman: I let the inconvenience of interruptions irritate me because they interfere with my plans and what I want to achieve. My agenda propels me into the day as I strive to meet my objectives and those that other people expect of me. Sometimes I feel like I am wearing blinders, much like those I used to see on my uncle's horses. I, too, stay focused. I, too, dare not look right or left lest I become distracted and drawn off course or slowed down.

Questions came with what I saw about myself: Is this really how I want to live? My heart is tight; my body is rigid while leaning into the next step. Is there a way I can meet my work expectations while I walk graciously through my days?

The interruption of the gospel word gave me an opportunity to examine some of my ways of thinking and acting and to change them when needed. In addition, I realized that setting priorities would help me know which activities get my attention and which interruptions get the response, "Wait until later." I felt that I, along with the woman who had approached and touched Jesus, had also been touched and was healed, at least a little.

At Times We Listen with Others

The plumbing in the main building of my monastery was on the verge of breaking down. We had not completely rewired the electrical system in 120 years. Open stairwells and an ineffective alarm system made the building a fire trap. Our insurance company declared its verdict: it would not renew our fire insurance unless we upgraded the building to meet safety standards. Our main building required not only a face lift but an overhaul.

We had known we needed to renovate, but we had other priorities and lacked money. Now, however, we had to take action. We needed to decide whether to demolish the building or renovate it. If we chose to renovate, what would we envision as its future purpose beyond our current housing and office needs? What room configurations would serve our vision for the future? How would we finance the project? After careful researching, numerous meetings of task teams and my monastic community at large, and much prayerful deliberation over many months, we decided that the best plan would be to renovate. We had faced and moved through many of our fears. We had developed a vision for the building. However, another hurdle stood before us: money.

More stress. Would it be feasible to conduct a capital campaign? More discernment followed, including a prayerful consideration of both cons and pros and the struggles to gain freedom from fear that would hinder making a wise decision. We had never conducted such a financial effort before. What would people think about our asking them for money? Most of our families are not well-off financially, so how could we ask them? Will a capital campaign make it appear that we are in financial trouble? It feels embarrassing to depend on others for money. Could we raise enough money through donations to cover the cost of the renovation; if not, what would we do? Who could serve on the advisory board for the campaign? After much prayerful deliberation, we decided to engage in a capital campaign.

Fast forwarding our story, yes, we chose architects and the construction company, developed designs and reworked them, structured the roles of sisters involved in overseeing the construction, delved into the activities of a capital campaign, and arranged alternate housing arrangements for the sisters who would be displaced for a year. The main building of our monastery now stands renewed and houses thirty-five sisters and several offices. Through the generosity of family and friends, we raised enough money to cover the costs of the renovation. Our listening, discernment, and consequent actions served us well. The building meets our current needs and embodies our vision for the future.

However, much more has happened to us than is apparent through the renovated monastery building. The renovation was *our* project. We accepted our responsibility to become informed on issues and progress reports. We listened to each other, often with struggles, to be attentive and respectful of varying views and feelings. We prayed, individually and communally. The measuring bar for patience was raised repeatedly and met often. We collaborated with many people and stretched our commitment to ourselves and the broader community as we visited with possible donors. Our vision for the future became clearer and more grounded. We have hoped, doubted, laughed, stumbled, and walked through frustration, and cheered various bits of good news.

How do we measure the long-term effects of these efforts and shifts within each of us? We can't. However, I trust that the inner renewal is as strong as the outer renovation. I again draw encouragement and affirmation from St. Benedict's reminder that through our living together, Christ "bring[s] us all together to everlasting life" (RB 72:12). Through our listening and its consequent discerning and responding, I myself have become more deeply convinced that this process of going to life everlasting together is occurring here and now. It happens in the daily round of activities in our lives.

Monastic communities are not the only arena for listening, discerning, and responding together. Groups such as families, staffs, teams, and councils are called to listen together. Life happens and gives people occasions to confer, listen to each other, and decide what to do in response. What might the family do for its summer vacation? What would be an effective agenda and process for a workshop a staff is planning? Should the city council affirm a request for rezoning? Decisions need to be made. To make them, participants might find it helpful to engage in processes similar to those my community experienced in renovating our building. Furthermore, what happens to the people involved is crucial: Is the influence constructive or destructive? For instance, does respect permeate the discussions? Are members open to the overall good of people involved or do special interests pull them into being close-minded and aggressive? Are qualities such as courage, justice, patience, and freedom of creativity key features of the dialogue? If so, the experience expands the hearts of the participants to include various people with their interests, ideas, and attitudes. Their hearts are open rather than constricted. Such are some of the marks of God's love in our midst.

The Disciple Is to Be Quiet and Listen

Chatter fills many of our days. People around me have news to tell, suggestions to make, and plans for an event. Sometimes the talk is essential; often it is part of the natural flow of the day. At times it drains my energy; sometimes it is invigorating. In addition to others speaking, I'm talking to myself—mulling over what to do next, wondering what one of my friends is doing, or planning my next class.

As good as the encounters of daily life may be, they can undermine my sense of inner balance. Furthermore, I have learned that when I'm overstimulated or am putting too much effort into holding my life together, I start to feel like a machine struggling to meet high standards of output. My natural capacity of intuition turns off, and my consciousness is desensitized to the movements of grace that come my way. I resist any more depletion of my attention, time, and energy. Thankfully, my spirit eventually rebels. It's had enough! But then what? Often I also am in a quandary: how can I honor the opportunities to give and receive while also caring for myself?

When I back off from activity for a bit, such as closing my office door so I do not hear my neighbors talking, a nearby vacuum cleaner whining, and doors opening and shutting, I intercept the energy drain from my psyche. I even sense that it stays within my office and me rather than being sucked outward. As I think about this self-preserving action, I realize the wisdom of Benedict's provision for silence and his urging that the "disciple is to be silent and listen" (RB 6:6). As I am quiet, I come home to myself for a while. As I become centered, I am able touch base with my purpose and make choices accordingly.

Quiet from outside and inside gives me inner space, whether momentary or longer, so I can listen to myself and what God is communicating to me. When I lean into momentary silences, I am given a chance to pause, notice, and choose. For example, a short pause after a homily or reading during worship helps me note some insights and possible responses available to me. At times during the day a phrase from the reading surfaces and it befriends me, reminding me of my few moments of conversation with God.

Fruits of quiet become available during the day because I can hear better. For example, the tone of my voice can catch my attention, reveal something about my attitude, and give me an opportunity to change it if I want to. I am open to one of my Benedictine sisters telling her lunch companions about her visit with her family; I loiter a little longer before going back to work.

A little hospitality at home goes a long way—for the sister telling stories and for those of us receiving them. I notice my reaction to the person driving the car that just cut in front of me; I realize that I am capable of allowing my anger to lead me to violence. I also get to choose to modify my response.

In embracing listening as a way of life, I find it essential that I surrender to longer periods of silence such as retreats, times when I am alone, daily times of prayer—especially for prayerful reading (*lectio divina*). The listening that occurs when I am quiet helps me ground my life in my relationship with Christ and deepen my commitment to live out of this relationship. I gain a deeper understanding of what it is for Christ to be my light and healer, the one who will not let me rest in mediocrity, the one who relentlessly pushes me toward love.

Quiet and reflection help me become more aware of the continual shower of blessings I am receiving all day long and throughout my life. In my awareness I can then receive them with responses such as gratitude, peace, courage, trust, and service. We also live with gentle expectation, trusting that blessings will be forthcoming. Dr. Rachel Remen, a psychiatrist immersed in the Jewish tradition, says, "We have been given many more blessings than we have received."[6] She recalls an image from one of her patients who said to her: we are "all being circled by our blessings, sometimes for years, like airplanes in a holding pattern at an airport, stacked up with no place to land. Waiting for a moment of our time, our attention."[7] Where are we when our blessings want to land, to be recognized, and to be appreciated?

Longer periods of quiet, such as a retreat for a couple days or a week, also help us to live reflectively, slowing down our pace of thinking and reacting, putting more time between the stimulus and our response. This pacing helps us gain some degree of freedom to choose more of our responses. We then respond rather than react. In moments of silence, the Spirit can slip in and give us at least a hint of insight and invitation along with the needed courage to respond as a disciple of Christ. Opportunities for quiet in daily life can be a normal part of every day or they can be selected periods of "time out": prayer alone and communal worship, stealing away to a nearby lake, walking or driving from one place to another in quiet, and enjoying the greens and flowers as we walk through a park. I find that the Spirit is quite adept at entering my life at such times, to at least quiet me so I can just be and can become more present in all the dynamics of my life.

The Buddhist monk Thich Nhat Hanh keeps me conscious of the value of mindfulness and of some of the hindrances we face in embracing it. Jon Frandsen says that Thich Nhat Hanh sees this attentiveness as "the full and complete awareness of life at this moment, whether one is washing dishes or playing with children . . . . Because mindfulness means paying attention to emotions and thoughts, our minds often race to the future or rake over the past to avoid being discomfited [in the present]."[8] Frandsen points out that Thich Nhat Hanh sees our over-involvement, our restlessness, and our flurry of thoughts giving way to constant activities. We "turn on television, pick up a novel, eat, have a drink because we do not want to go home to ourselves."[9]

I have found that often people do not like quiet. Some admit that they need to turn on the radio immediately when entering their car. Others say they are addicted to their iPod with its music and videos and to their cell phones that give easy access to e-mails and text messages. Some are uneasy when they are alone in their apartment without the television on. They feel restless, lonely, as if something is missing. When we feel these reactions to quiet, it is difficult to befriend it. It is experienced as negative. We feel it needs to be avoided at almost any cost. Our fast-paced and multidirectional life tells us that being quiet is abnormal or a waste of time. Furthermore, our communications often come to us through sound bytes and text messaging. Movies and television programs that move abruptly and quickly from one scene to another. Hence, we are denied a possible emotional impact. We skim over the surface of emotions and jump through the parts of the plot without much involvement. Our emotional responsiveness is siphoned away.

Listening as a reflective way of life, lived within the context of the gospel, increases the possibilities of doing our part to bring the reign of God's love to greater fullness. Listening, guided by the Spirit and supported by skills of discerning what we hear as options for the formation of our attitudes and actions, helps us respond to situations with the direction we choose. Our capacities such as our emotions, memory, imagination, reason, and will call for listening; they serve as messengers of possibilities. Furthermore, this way of living within the dailiness of our lives gradually enlarges our hearts to meet and welcome God in God's many entrances into our lives. We become practiced disciples of God.

Chapter 5

Stability:
We Stand as We Walk

. . . love one another deeply from the heart. You have been born anew . . . through the living and enduring word of God. (1 Pet 1:22b-23)

Crossing the Street Together

During my late afternoon commute home, I sat in my usual seat in the front row on the #61 city bus in Pittsburgh. The bus slowed to a stop at the red light near the Carnegie Museum of Natural History. Two people were crossing the street with the go ahead of the "walk" light. The woman hobbled as fast as she could, her head cocked so she could watch the traffic light. She held on to the arm of a large-framed man who walked firmly, defying the dangers of the traffic. I marveled to myself: "How lucky that woman is to have someone to hang onto."

Then I noticed the man's white cane. He moved it carefully so he could detect possible interferences. He walked steadily while the woman, clutching his arm as she watched the light, directed their trek across the street.

I felt a shift of perspective, what some would call an "aha" moment. Stability for the woman was based both in her ability to see and in the firm stance of her escort. A white cane and the seeing eyes of his partner gave the man some sense of safety. Together they made their way through a threat to both of them.

Together they embodied two basic dynamics essential for our lives: stability and movement. Both needed to move; both lacked capabilities for a successful crossing of the street alone; each offered an ability to the partner. Grounded in trust of each other, they were able to risk moving onto a dangerous street. What would they have done without each other?

This incident sparked questions for me: When do I need help "to cross the street"? Whose "arm" do I clutch? On whom do I lean? Who helps me see where I'm to go? When am I unstable? On what is my stability grounded? What does my stability enable me to do? What possibilities does my instability offer me?

Stability Is Here and Now

Stability stands on its own feet on solid ground. It helps us to stay put rather than shift to whatever lures us. However, it is flexible, not rigid, so we can respond to situations. We know stability when we meet it. For instance, when I am talking with someone who is stable within herself, I feel she is present to me and I am present to her. Recently I conversed with Sister Suzanne, a ninety-seven-year-old member of my monastic community. She asked: "Why am I still living when my siblings and many of my nieces and nephews have died?" Almost in the same breath she said: "Because of my ministry. I give to my family and other people by listening to them [often by phone] and praying for them. They seem to feel comfortable in talking with me, sometimes for an hour at a time." Sister Suzanne is at home with herself. I felt at home with her. She is at home with her purpose in life—as a monastic in her community and in her service to others. She is at peace with her past. From her inner home she reaches out to others, and in this instance, to me. She expects blessings in the future, especially in her arrival at her ultimate home.

Reflecting later on my encounter with Sister Suzanne, I realized that I had met God as "I am who I am" (Exod 3:14). Sister Suzanne's presence to herself and to me gave me a glimpse of one aspect of what it is to be in the image and likeness of God. In her way, she said, "I am. I am who I am." Furthermore, she offered me space to enter and be myself. I also felt that I was drawn into God's hospitality and stability—God's faithful presence—through her. The veil that often hinders my recognition became more transparent. I met God through this encounter in my daily life.

We need to be available to the work of the Spirit. When we evade what is given to us here and now, especially when uncomfortable, we are "gone" when we need to be "home." Stability helps us stay put. For instance, as Joan persists in her studies rather than repeatedly responding to e-mails and text messaging, the quality of her work improves. The discipline will also strengthen her inner resources of patience and perseverance. Joe struggles with his neighbor's complaining. Nothing is right. Joe's attempts to move to a constructive stance are intercepted with "yes, but . . ." How long is time enough for Joe to try to listen? Is there any way to change the perspective of a person who negates incessantly? Joe perseveres for a while in being respectful and eventually lets go of his expectations that he can "fix" the negativity blowing his way. He is at peace; he did what he could. Mike regularly weeds, cultivates, and trims his garden, and enjoys the opening of the flowers. Then comes the picking of the first sweet corn—more delight. Brenda has moved into a new job. It is exciting and she brings many skills, but she feels overwhelmed, vulnerable, and afraid people will think she's incompetent. After some weeks of struggle, she meets with a friend to talk. She gains some new perspectives, highlights her abilities, and learns additional ways of relating to her new circumstances. Showing up regularly for her time of quiet prayer enables the daily Scripture readings to be kneaded into Kathy's heart. She leaves more attuned to the principles she wants to guide her interpretations and actions.

In such instances, individuals are physically and consciously present to the people, things, and activities happening in their daily lives. Shifts occur within them. The changes expand their hearts so they can take in more of life than they could if they were embedded in the easy way that enables them to avoid discomfort and pain. Furthermore, people in the incidents described above are giving love through dynamics such as listening, patience, being open to positive perspectives and relationships, delighting in nature's wonders, admitting vulnerability, and reaching out for help. From the perspective of the Christian faith journey, they are participating in the dying and rising of Christ. Their openhearted responses require letting go of those responses that are self-serving. No wonder people resist staying put and entering into the situation. A kind of dying is required. But then there is another perspective, one of promise and hope. While letting go, people are growing into a fuller expression of their true self that wants to live with purpose and values that help them be more loving and creative in the world. At heart they continue Christ's mission: to bring to fullness God's love in all parts of creation.

Many years ago Demetrius Dumm, OSB, expressed an image that spoke to me of our tendency to avoid the pain of change and some of the effects of this evasion. We are like a block of marble on a platform supported by wheels.[1] Whenever the sculptor tries to hit the marble, it moves and the hit either misses its mark entirely or is off focus. This image presents a snapshot of me. My wheels work very well as the Sculptor tries to release the shape hidden in me. I stay busy so I am not available for the work of the chisel and hammer that calls for awareness and reflection. I resist what I fear and skirt around it. I evade the discomfort of trying to resolve a conflict. I want to stop working on a project when I become discouraged with it and the people I am working with. I need to remove my wheels so I can gain the stability that allows me to be present when the blows come. Then maybe I will begin to see more of the image of Christ being released in me, bit by bit.

Stability Is Poised

Stability is not rigid or a place of safety from the discomfort of change. It is alive and fluid and somewhat relaxed and flexible. It enables us to be poised and alert to respond to new possibilities. Much like bamboo that sways in the wind, we can withstand the winds of our days without breaking, cracking, or twisting. Similarly, skyscrapers have enough flexibility to allow them to move in the wind, thus avoiding twisting and even collapse when buffeted by high winds and earthquakes. The ability to move enables them to return to dynamic equilibrium, or flexible stability. Similarly, our stability needs to be poised to move while being grounded.

I cannot predict what will enter my day. Relaxed and flexible stability accompanied by mindfulness will poise me to make an appropriate response, one I have chosen. Sometimes the event that breaks into the usual course of our lives is dramatic. For instance, Beth and Jim have welcomed their first baby. And they have also birthed major shifts in their family. New stressors of time, finances, and relationships are challenging them. Life feels crazy, and assurances that the reactions are normal do not help alleviate their situation. It still feels crazy. They are buffeted by questions: How can they continue to do all they did before the baby came while assuming new responsibilities? It's expensive to birth and care for a baby; how can the expenses be covered? How do Mom and Dad welcome their newcomer and sustain their relationship with each other? How does Mom regain some degree of normalcy when her hormones are pulling her into unfamiliar and disorienting moods?

In such circumstances, the characters in the drama get to draw from their inner and outer resources as they adjust and seek a new equilibrium. They may require support from community members, family, neighbors, and coworkers. The overall experience offers many opportunities for the chisel of the Sculptor to strike and evoke responses such as patience, more dependence on others, creative thinking, perseverance, reconciliation, humor, and joy. Those involved can release more fully the image of God that they are.

A community that is poised responds well to stability. For example, when my monastic community engages in visioning and planning processes, one result is a deeper confidence that we are walking on solid ground. We gain a stronger sense of who we are and what our direction will be in the future. However, we also need to be aware that while we discern a basic direction and make some plans, there are many unforeseen outside factors that will affect us: the stock market can drop, the cost of food and gas can gouge the budget unexpectedly, or someone in a key position can become seriously ill. However, favorable winds can blow also. A significant donation could enable us to move ahead on a project sooner than planned. Thus our planning sets a direction for fulfilling our mission and using our resources while at the same time being poised enough to respond to whatever will occur within our community and the broader civic, national, and global communities. Our vision calls us forward and holds the space for carrying out our purpose while allowing varying circumstances to be embraced.

St. Benedict: Focus on Stability Through Daily Events of Life

St. Benedict provides a guide that calls for structures and practices to help us confront our hearts that want to wander off, seeking something we judge to be better than what is here and now. He deplored the gyrovagues, monks "who spend their entire lives drifting from region to region, staying as guests for three or four days in different monasteries" (RB 1:10). Benedict calls this a "disgraceful way of life" because it prevents them from settling down and finding freedom from their own will and appetites (RB 1:11-12). His guide for living the gospel calls for a commitment to a specific place and a way of life within a particular community (RB 58; 4:78). Monastics are gradually initiated into a specific monastery where they make a promise to live the rest of their lives according to the gospel, Benedict's guide, and the tradition of the community. They become grounded and grow roots in a particular place, which frees them to enter into the work of seeking God in all situations of their lives.

As noted previously, St. Benedict established "a school [or workshop] for the Lord's service" where the dynamics of turning the heart to God through daily conversion can occur (RB Prol 45-49; RB 4). How does this turning happen? We monastics are to bring respect and graciousness to washing the dishes, serving meals, cooking, and handling things. Benedict says we should provide care for the sick as if they were Christ. Work is to be part of everyone's daily life. We live with some degree of routine through a regular schedule of prayer, work, community gatherings, sleep, and leisure. Our lives are not dramatic with many crises or ecstatic experiences of God that we often think will make life more interesting and significant.[2] It does not take long after we enter the monastery for our first expectations of the mystique of monastic life to be slowly chipped away. The routine and structures can become boring and stressful. The monastic community is a cross section of humanity. There is a variety of personalities, needs and skills, and degrees of compatibility. We are drawn to some people; some we want to avoid. The disillusioning process through which we let go of the idyllic view of the monastery opens us to greater availability to the action of the Spirit, for whom the daily life of people is a significant workshop. Our feet become more firmly planted on the ground. We become more stable for the daily work of life.

The monastery provides a way of life that helps monastics learn how to live as persons committed to God. Early in his rule, Benedict outlines the tools for good works (RB 4). They offer a guide for Christian life. In a way, the reader will find nothing new. The tools can already be found in Scripture. The monastic's life is to be grounded in the baptismal commitment to live as Christ in the world today and to help transform the world. Hence, Scripture is our foundational guide. St. Benedict's first words in the listing of the tools of the monastery root us in Christ's perspective and the goal of our vocation: love of God, self, and neighbor as well as of all creation (RB 4:1-2). The context of the rule repeatedly draws us to the faithful living of the gospel in our everyday encounters. This goal is central and inspires commitment. However, our conversion to a fuller expression of Christ through our fidelity to monastic life is so gradual and questionable that it is often challenging for us to believe anything constructive is occurring. At times we might well say, "Is this all there is?"

Is This All There Is?

"Is this all there is?" is a question that sometimes haunts us. It was a foundational question for Pippin, son of Charlemagne, who, in the 1972 Broadway musical *Pippin*, grapples with finding meaning in the routine and insignificant activities of his daily life.[3] This struggle drives him to squander many of his years and energy in seeking fulfillment through riches, sex, and power. Pippin marries Catherine; they have a son. Still his heart is restless. He expects that happiness awaits him somewhere other than where he is. After some years of marriage, Pippin again moves on because he feels he is extraordinary and so cannot give his time repeatedly to the daily stuff of his life. He is made for bigger things. Catherine quietly confronts Pippin's aspirations, asking him what makes him so sure he is made for grandeur.[4]

Pippin's desperation and frenzied search for experiences that are spectacular, new, stimulating, and extraordinary demonstrate a search for God that has gone awry. He seeks his ultimate happiness here and now, but his feet are not grounded on the earth. Pippin is on the move, unwilling to stop and let the interactions of daily life touch and form him and bring him joy. He has not caught on that boredom, repetition, and the gradual wearing away of visions of self-grandeur could bring him wisdom. He measures vitality by being emotionally charged. Then he feels alive and, at times, even heroic. Pippin is deaf to some of the gnawing questions of life we all face: Who am I? Where am I going? What am I a part of? Am I significant? How do I make meaning out of my life? Why do I feel so listless and unsatisfied when I haven't accomplished much during the day? And a haunting question remains for Pippin as he wonders whether or not his life that seems so ordinary is all there is.

While Pippin presents us with a caricature, I see myself and others in him. I want to escape what seems commonplace, what I judge to be ordinary pursuits, my daily routine and people, for something more exciting. My fear of boredom and feeling insignificant can stir up a desire for drama or crisis. Who am I without a juicy story to tell or crisis to resolve? Am I addicted to the story and adrenalin rush that gives my identity illusory importance? Do I need to be hyper to feel alive?

What messages from our society, particularly through advertising, contribute to our dissatisfaction, unrealistic expectations, and sense of entitlement to what is better and best? What fantasies, mental scheduling of activities, and imaginings related to our various projects lure us out of offering our presence and efforts to our current relationships and projects? How do our possibilities for mobility, such as car transportation and a few clicks that take us into cyberspace, challenge our being "at home" to ourselves and other people? From where do we get our expectations that we should be treated as special and that we are entitled to make demands of those who are serving us? In what ways has our becoming disconnected from the land hindered us from exercising our responsibility for the earth while promoting the expectation that we should have the foods we want when we want them regardless of the distance they need to be transported? How can I move into awareness and freedom so I am better able to choose which urgings I will follow?

I have found that reflection and allowing my restless heart to have a voice help to root me in my basic vocation: to seek God. It is good for me to know by experience that I will not be ultimately satisfied by any person, thing, or experience while on this earth. I take courage from St. Augustine: "You have made us for yourself, Lord, and our hearts are restless until they rest in you."[5] No wonder the daily stuff of life often seems trite and inconsequential, yet at the same time I enjoy beauty even in the simplest of things, am deeply moved by a sense of the sacred in silence, nature, a child, and feel pulled beyond myself. My heart finds joy and I want more. My heart is big enough to open to more than the ordinary circumstances of life. It is expanded enough to find "the more" in my everyday life. And yet, even these fulfill-ments of my yearning are not the ultimate end of my desire. Before long, I am restless and seeking again. This dissatisfaction and searching are essential to being human. Through them God draws the human heart to God's own self.

And so, we return to the question: "Is this all there is?" At such times of questioning, humility and courage are required for us to hear the answers, yes and no. One voice expresses its answer in words such as the following:

> Yes, this is all there is. And each encounter with a person, thing, or event gives you an opportunity to meet God and respond in some expression of love. This is where you can die and rise with Christ. This is where the transformation of your heart awaits you. Yes, your search for feeling significant will be frustrated, but right in your here and now is where God will meet you and nudge your heart to greater openness so you can love better. Yes, this is all there is. Isn't it extraordinary? Wonderful! Isn't it awesome that this is *all* there is—so much, so wonder-filled! Your daily life is a signifi-cant place for the *mirabilia Dei*, the wonders of God, to occur.

Another voice accompanies the first one:

> No, this is not all there is. There is more. Do not settle for what is limited, partially and temporarily satisfying. Keep your thirst-ing, hungering, and longing piqued. While you enjoy much in your life, you were created for more; you exist for God. Let your prayer be that of some of the psalms: "As the deer longs for streams of water, so my soul longs for you, O God. My being thirsts for God, the living God. When can I go and see the face of God?" (Ps 118:174-176). And live your responsibility to help keep the yearning of other seekers alive and focused on what will bring them to God.

Both voices encourage us to walk in the dynamic tension of standing as we walk forward in daily life. Stability that is poised to respond to God's daily invitations will support us so we can listen, discern, and move to our next step.

Grounded in Community

I have often heard the image of a deep-rooted tree used to exemplify stability. The roots hold the tree firmly; the weight, height, and many branches of the tree are depending on the security of the roots. Recently I added another dimension to this image when I learned the ways of redwood trees in California. The trees grow in a circle of six to seven trees; their roots are intertwined. At times, the saplings draw nourishment and strength from the parent tree's root system. A mature redwood has a root system that is only about ten to thirteen feet deep, with a width of about sixty to eighty feet. Stability is gained through the roots that are entangled with neighboring ones.

We, too, do not live and develop alone. We need companions who support and challenge us, who can be counted on to be there with and for us, and who are on a journey similar to ours. We experience similar dynamics and bring the energy of purpose and resoluteness to each other. We, too, come from a common life source. We are kin to each other. As one of my brothers repeatedly reminds us, his siblings, "It's all about family!" True, and our challenge is to hold a big enough view of family to include all people and all creation.

As we list the communities in which we participate, we will come up with more than one. Some of mine are family, monastic community, various circles of friends, college campus community, my department at work, the local city, and national and international communities. Members are current and past; they continue to inspire and support me. Although they have died, Mom and Dad frequently are my companions. My monastic foremothers inspire me with the stories of their lives and ongoing presence. I never leave a visit to our cemetery without being energized to face the challenges and live the purpose of my life. I know of some of the hardships and the determination of these sisters. It seems that by standing on the ground around them, I absorb some of their energy, and they come with me as I leave.

My monastic sisters and I are part of the local community, a membership that calls for various involvements, such as planning for the future land development of our city, civic issues, and relationships with businesses. I note here a relationship that has developed more recently. Our food service personnel search out products that we can purchase locally and that are produced without chemicals. Also, we are growing many of our vegetables without the use of pesticides. Each of these connections strengthens the roots of community in our area, while at the same time individual producers of various commodities are supported. Together, we stand respectfully on the earth and support each other's healthy living.

In addition to standing on the sacred ground of our past and its influence today, my community also projects into the future. We are integral to the future; the future is already with us and draws us toward it. For instance, people's growing thirst for support on their spiritual journeys evokes discernment and planning for how we monastics might help meet these yearnings through services such as spiritual companioning and retreat opportunities, providing ways people can affiliate with us as a monastic community, and collaborating with others in projects. We are beginning to explore how we might use technology to help us connect with others. Who we are and what we do now will serve the common good of the future.

The purpose of each community is unique. The degree of intimacy within each and the strength of the members' commitment vary. The ways of incorporation differ. However, the stability offered by communities helps the members walk their life journey with the good of themselves and others at heart.

Grounded in God

I know deeply that God is the source of my strength. Even when my trust wavers, my faith that God is present, that God cares, and that God's loving vision will win out over numerous threats to it keeps my feet on the ground as I walk step by step. I see providential events and patterns in my life that make sense. For example, as the oldest in a family of eight children I was prepared for living many aspects of Benedictine community. I knew what it was to share household responsibilities. I knew how to share material goods and to wait my turn. Our large garden fed the family and provided a primary work activity for all of us. Through this work I was given some special gifts. I learned that each food has its season and that the movement from planting to harvest takes time. As much as I love strawberries, I knew they would not accompany me into July. Our garden also taught me that, although we invest time and energy in it, the results are not entirely up to us. Healthy garden growth and harvesting require good seeding, enough water, good soil, enough time for the plant to grow and flourish, and someone to harvest the food. If any of these variables is missing, the crop will suffer.

My childhood and later experiences also taught me that God is the source of life and growth. Awareness of such providence helps me trust that God has been with me all along the way. God has been stable in God's faithfulness. These lessons help me relate with myself and others so I can more readily let go of expectations of a quick fix for situations I want to improve. Furthermore, God is the chief Gardener, so I had better rely on God for what I need. God was the ground of my life before I came into being and before I became aware of God. God has gone before me. So I have a basis to trust that God is here now—with me and our world—and will be in the future.

This confidence is developed and supported by living in awareness and discernment while reflecting on life as it is revealing itself in our daily experiences. When we are present to what is happening at any time, our senses are active and enable us to participate in the encounter. We might realize someone (God and people around us) is giving us a gift, and we receive it graciously. The smell and feel of rain, the disturbing questions of a teenager who wonders whether he will live to become an adult, the taste of the first radishes of the season, the soothing feel of a cat's fur along with the vibration of the purring motor under it, the smell of a hospital, and the face of a friend that we meet unexpectedly remind us of the gifts available when we are attuned to life as it is occurring. As we live mindfully, we will develop the art of walking through our days with open hands to receive whatever comes our way, even though at first we resist it. We do not know what is hidden behind what we perceive. More and more our responses to such encounters will be a thank you to people and to God, sometimes even before we know what will be revealed.

Being aware of God's action in our daily experiences can help us recognize that God is here now. This awareness enables me to know God as a constant companion and friend who walks with me. I am reminded of some of my mom and dad's love letters I read recently. During much of the two years before they married, Mom lived in Minnesota, Dad in Montana. Their letters were endearing messages that later brought me into the private and sacred space of their relationship. I also read about harvesting, haying, going to local parties, encounters with neighboring farmers, family activities, and tasks done in the hospital where Mom worked. Nothing seemed too trite to write about. They seemed to want to share in order to bring their lives together.

When people are significant to each other, so, too, is whatever happens in their lives. Such is the nature of intimacy. I have found this to be true in my relationship with God and God's with me. Awareness of God's daily, provident presence allows and encourages me to know God's personal love for me. True, God is transcendent, beyond my comprehension. Such a God can protect and bring goodness and life out of what I see as negative and dying experiences. God's love is also beyond my comprehension as it is revealed event by event, even what I judge to be mundane. As I've come to know this personal love, I've grown in trust that within the routine of my life, there is a current of care that frequently carries me along. I also trust that since God expresses love in what I consider ordinary and mundane events, my responses in such situations are significant to God. I stand in faith that God is with all of us in the everyday-ness of life, that God gives us moments of intimacy and then slips back into being quietly present and unnoticed. The God I know connects with us in this way.

At times the world beyond us becomes unstable in ways that severely threaten our personal stability, and our foundation of trust is rocked because it is difficult to see God's faithful presence among us. Wars cause devastation to land, civilians, and trust among nations; often they seem senseless and overwhelm us with grief. We question, "Where is God?" Ecological crises, disregarded by many, bring those who care face-to-face with challenges to hope. Economic predicaments that bring severe hardships to those not causing them reek of injustice and powerlessness. Can God even make right what we have made so wrong? Natural disasters bring major disruptions to people, nature, and many facets of life. Where is God who is supposed to be all powerful?

While the answers regarding how to regain stability are complex and require time to find and carry out, we need to remain grounded as much as we can in our daily lives where God will continue to be revealed in the whispers of the everyday. It is here that we can serve as God's heart, hands, feet, and eyes.[6] Here is where God is continuing to become human in each of us. It is here and now that we carry out the urging of the psalmist: "Let us open our eyes to the light that comes from God, and our ears to the voice from heaven that every day calls out this charge: *If you hear his voice today, do not harden your hearts* (Ps 94 [95]:8)" (RB Prol 9). Hearing God's voice and receiving God's light, even if bit by bit, can bring us stability. This stability serves as the launching place for action in the immediate and broader dimensions of our world. We can also stand in the conviction that because I am here, God is here. Because God is here, I am stable; I am significant; I can make a difference. I can join with the Spirit in moving all creation to a greater fullness of God's love.

Chapter 6

The Dramatic Ordinary: For Those Who Groan

"Because the poor are despoiled, because the needy groan,
  I will now rise up," says the LORD;
"I will place them in the safety for which they long."

(Ps 12:5)

At Times We Groan

All of us are hurting about something. Some are whimpering. Some are groaning. Some are suffering so deeply no sound can express it. Some of us are in crisis. Some are walking with others through theirs.

Regardless of the causes and seeming extraordinariness of crises, they are ordinary occurrences. They are ordinary, literally reordering, opportunities through which we can seek God, shift our perspectives, undergo a change of heart, and make choices that bring conversion into our daily life. We then move through dying to rising into some degree of new life. A crisis can also slam into us so forcefully that our emotions shut down and we are unable to make thoughtful responses, at least temporarily. We need to rely on others to help us move through the crisis, especially in its early steps, as we put one foot in front of another.

Crisis Claims a Life of Its Own

About twelve years ago a crisis ambushed me and left me in a desert for several months. I had returned to teaching at the

College of Saint Benedict in the fall after a leave of absence for several years during which I served as prioress of my monastic community. During these years in leadership I had grown accustomed to relating with adults, ages thirty and older. We had planned projects and implemented steps to realize them. I had been involved with boards of four institutions. I had walked with many people through personal goal setting and crisis management. Consulting and collaborating with people around the United States were part of my daily life. Life was vibrant and I felt fully involved in it.

When the six years of this involvement and service were completed, I eagerly returned to teaching at Saint Ben's, where I had taught for several years before becoming prioress. This teaching had been a grounding source of purpose and joy for me. But a disturbing surprise awaited me, and it didn't take long for me to start groaning. I had entered a desert where the weather was stormy, the landscape stark, and where I needed to make my way without a map and with only a few landmarks available.

The constant depth of questioning without any clarity or openings carried me into a whirlpool of confusion. Why was I not energized by teaching as I had been? Why did my world seem so small? Why was I so short-tempered with my students? Why was I not sleeping well? Why was I not feeling like myself? During the four months of the fall semester, I fumbled my way through responsibilities that previously had been familiar and comfortable. My doubt about my ability to teach gradually ate away at my confidence. I felt lonely; several of the faculty and staff I was accustomed to seeing were not around anymore. Except for a few close friends, I felt too embarrassed to expose my difficulties to members of my monastic community. After all, I was known as an effective teacher.

I cried often. Some days I couldn't eat; some days I ate too much. I felt that my life was out of my control. Some days I reflected on what was going on; other days I didn't dare think about it. No matter what I did, I could not escape my pain.

About a month into the semester I recognized that I was going through a major transition that for me had become a crisis. Its symptoms were evident and nameable. It became clear that I was experiencing what William Bridges calls disidentification: I didn't feel like myself, particularly in the classroom and among my colleagues.[1] The people and students I'd known before and to whom I'd hoped to return had changed. Some faculty members had retired and had been replaced by new ones. The students with whom I'd related before had graduated. I had returned to the college without my former identity. Furthermore, I realized I was grieving the loss of the people with whom I had been involved in various organizations and services during my years as prioress. I was not able to maintain my previous relationships with them; my sense of who I was through activities with these people was gone.

My disidentification was complicated by disillusionment.[2] My hopes and what I envisioned for my return disintegrated. My usual ways of dealing with such conditions were not working. One-to-one conversations did little to establish a relationship with the students. Assessing my assignments and modifying them in ways I thought would be helpful failed to stop the complaints about them. I tried a greater variety of activities to engage the students: role playing, debating, more student-designed and student-led discussions. Nothing I did "fixed" the students, me, or the situation. And there seemed to be no end in sight. I was left to cope as well as I could and wait. Some light came when I realized I needed to receive help and gifts as they came to me: a day without major tension in the classroom, a word of encouragement from a friend, or a creative approach to a lesson plan.

I felt disoriented.[3] I didn't know where I was going. Am I an effective teacher? If I can't teach anymore, what will I do? I wanted to quit, to run away. I pulled back from engaging in most relationships, especially with my students. I didn't care much about anything. I moved more and more into disengagement.[4]

Fortunately I knew something about the dynamics of transition. I had taught courses on the topic. Now I needed to walk my own journey through this major shift. My knowledge gave me some stepping stones on which I could secure my feet. However, I still needed to walk through the pain of it, day by day. Some days those stones felt slippery and treacherous. I was in between what I knew during my former identity and work, both as a college teacher and as prioress, and what was now new. I knew I wasn't crazy. I wasn't a failure. And I could begin to let go of my expectation that I should be coping better.

Disillusionment and disorientation truly blindsided me. I walked back into my college life confident that I would continue as I had before. I knew what to expect. I knew how to teach. I'd taught the courses before. I had not prepared myself for what came my way. I was caught unaware and felt influences coming from surprising directions.

In contrast, while I faced challenges when I became prioress, I did not feel caught off guard. I knew this role would be different from anything I had ever experienced. I expected a high learning curve. I foresaw that I would be vulnerable and that I would make judgments and decisions that would not always be the best. This knowledge of my fledgling status and attempts to move wisely were not only mine. The members of my monastic community were conscious of my situation, too. They gave me expectations that matched my beginning steps. They also helped me limit my expectations of myself. Thus, I did not face disillusionment and disidentification as I did when I returned to teaching. As a beginning prioress, I bore no identity and expectations to protect. I, as well as others, presumed I would need time to gain competence and to put on a public face.

Supports along the Way

While I drew help from my understandings of transition throughout the four months of the fall semester, I also gained support from some other resources. One was my friend Martha, who held my head above water and kept me from drowning. I could risk being a mess in her presence; I could return to her as often as I needed, sometimes talking about the same struggles and feelings each time. She listened and offered comments and suggestions that helped me in situations where I could not see well enough to interpret and respond wisely.

I recall a shift when one of Martha's comments helped me realize that sometimes such painful experiences happen; they are an ordinary part of life. I sensed myself letting go of my resistance to walk this journey that was given to me. I began to surrender to it and relate to it in my attitudes as constructively as I could. Throughout the semester, I felt Martha's care when I didn't feel I could give much to myself. This ground helped me maintain my footing. Martha's support helped me see well enough to take at least the immediate steps ahead of me.

Another support was physical exercise, which allowed me to release pent-up energy and relax my muscles. In addition, recalling that in the past I had been an effective teacher gradually gave me hope that eventually I would return to my usual self and expertise in this role. Also, remembering other challenging situations that I'd lived through helped me to trust that I would come through this one safely and I'd return to my normal self. I grew to believe that I wouldn't have to give up teaching.

I also gained reassurance about myself when I realized that I was in a very difficult teaching situation. One of my three classes met on alternate days at 8:00 a.m. and was composed mostly of first-year students who strutted into class with their high school mentality of being at the top of the student hierarchy; after coasting through their high school classes, many ignored the need to give time and energy to studying. Furthermore, about halfway through the semester, I learned that several students were dealing with issues of depression (and I probably was, too). Students in another class were unruly and hard to tame and move into a learning mode. While I was not at my best in relating with the students, these participants were contributing to the dynamics of the classes, too. It wasn't only my fault. I responded affirmatively to an inner invitation to forgive myself for my failures with the students and my perceived failure in not meeting my expectations.

Some days I felt God was close; on others I felt isolated from God—and everyone else. At times the beginning words of the Liturgy of Hours were all I could pray: "O God, come to my assistance." Sometimes I was Jacob wrestling with God and life personified as an adversary (see Gen 32:22-32). Neither would let go, and I'd go limping into another day. At other times I clung to consoling reminders through words such as those in Psalms 5 and 103 that I applied to myself:

> Give ear to my words, O LORD;
> give heed to my sighing.
> Listen to the sound of my cry,
> my king and my God!
> for to you I pray.
> O LORD, in the morning you hear my voice;
> in the morning I plead my case to you, and watch. (Ps 5:1-3)

> The LORD is merciful and gracious. . . .
> . . . the steadfast love of the LORD is from everlasting to
> everlasting. (103:8a, 17a)

When I looked back later, I saw that my trust in God as caring and as journeying with me in the desert helped me keep going. God was with me. I found God's tangible and caring presence through the strength I received to go to class every day and through people, friends, and members of my monastic community. They did not need to do or say anything extraordinary or relate to my experience. Their authentic involvement in everyday activities and interactions with each other and with me were enough. I learned more deeply that God is faithful; my trust grew stronger.

A Long Day in and out of the Desert

The intensity and duration of my transition contributed to its becoming a significant experience. I forced myself to give attention to what was going on and to reflect, alone and with others, on what I noticed. Later I realized that I had been engaged in a process of transformation, of dying and rising to some new life in Christ.

As I experienced my vulnerability, especially physically and emotionally, I was compelled to let go of my long-standing pattern of self-sufficiency and reach out to other people for help. I knew I could not make it through the semester through my own efforts alone. I didn't like this feeling of being vulnerable. I was not in control. While resisting dependence, I also appreciated receiving care and developing relationships with people. The ambivalence of resisting and welcoming support felt unnerving. I began to realize that feeling my vulnerability was a gift, and my hands gradually opened to befriend it. I gained some degree of freedom from my public and self-image that called relentlessly for performing well in what I was doing. I also tried to live in the present moment and to note and respond to what was happening at the time rather than interpreting it in the framework of my worries.

Humility became a close companion of vulnerability. I got to stand in the truth of both my limitations and my gifts. Humility led me to plant my feet on the earth outside the limelight of my own and others' opinions. I admitted that I was not the effective teacher I had been before. This realization brought me to question who I really was. In time I realized that I am more than a successful teacher; this role is only one aspect of my identity. I'm also a person who loves nature and enjoys fun; I especially like to photograph scenes as well as incidental objects that might be overlooked. I am a faithful friend, loyal in times of joy and suffering. I am significant to my family and my monastic community. I can be counted on to show up for gatherings, care about and listen to individuals, and contribute to my monastic sisters' daily life by helping to wash dishes, husk sweet corn, and communicate about family news. I became more grounded in humility as I claimed my strengths as well as my limitations.

Through my crisis I became more able to realize and accept my limitations and my gifts, whose presence had become overshadowed by my brokenness. I also grew in a deeper conviction that while I needed to lean on other people, I am not a helpless victim. Rather, I am interdependent, needing to give to and receive from others. Being humbled enabled me to stand more authentically and effectively in the truth of who I am and who I am in my interrelationship with others, God, and all of creation. Through this grounding I am empowered to live authentically with new criteria to measure who I am and the success of my efforts.

I received the gift of a greater awareness of the integration of my body and its impact on my coping capabilities. Having been able previously to push my body to do whatever I thought I needed to do, I often took it for granted. My body was usually available at my beck and call. However, when lack of sleep and emotional pain started to gnaw at my energy and sense of well-being, I realized I could not take my physical self for granted or push relentlessly toward my objectives. My physical being finally became a respected friend.

Gratitude for the first semester emerged during the spring semester. I was grateful that some transition to peace and effectiveness in teaching and relating to other people and to myself gradually returned. I also walked in gratitude for what I'd gained through my previous semester. Through the crisis my relationship with God deepened. Even when I felt desolate and that God was far away, I clung to the trust that God was somehow present. I became more sensitive in detecting even the hints of God's continual presence, and I remained attentive for more. A cheerful greeting from a student, an affirmation from a colleague, waking up without a headache, a sunny day, a lighthearted quip from a friend, and an evocative phrase from Scripture during prayer were received as personal gifts. As I reviewed the semester, I became more aware that many of the events of daily life helped me walk through the long event of crisis. Thankfulness became an expansive attitude of heart as I recognized and acknowledged the dynamics and people along the way of my trek through the desert.

As a result of weathering the trials of the semester, I grew in inner stamina, especially perseverance, resilience, courage, and hope. I also developed new understandings about crises and the possibilities they offer. Life served as a "school," and I learned many valuable lessons about dying and rising in Christ that I can now share with others through listening, questions, and offering perspectives. St. Benedict has it right when he refers to the monastery, indeed, all of life, as "a school for the Lord's service"—a school where we learn to see with God's vision and to love (RB Prol 45). The learning for all Christians, as well as monastics, in the school of life is from the inside out. While we come to know objectively, we also learn to know by heart and through the heart. This wisdom undergirds and permeates who we are and what we do.

St. Benedict also supports this type of learning through crisis and the routine of life for the development of wise persons who can instruct others by word and example. He says that the teachers of others need to have developed "goodness of life and wisdom in teaching" (RB 64.2; cf. 21.4 on deans). The experiences of life give them revelations of God's loving presence and guidance as well as provide the chiseling through daily encounters that helps release the image of Christ they are. In addition to becoming wise through the processes of life's invitations and responses, they have learned how to "read" events. In turn, they are responsible for helping others learn these skills. This circular dynamic of learning and teaching others by words and example is a calling for all of us (cf. RB 2).

Here I am reminded of Lynn and her experience when she participated in a conference based on how to live through constructive suffering. After one of the presentations an older woman leaned over to Lynn, a friend of the speaker, and asked if the speaker had suffered much during her life.

"No," replied Lynn.

The woman went on to say, "I thought so. I can tell by the way she is talking about suffering that she has not experienced much pain. She is too theoretical and detached. I don't hear much of the pathos that comes with suffering."

Lynn asked, "Are you going to say something to her about your observation?"

"No—life will teach her."

Yes, life, everyday experiences and dramatic ones of pain and joy, will teach all of us. Life will chip away what hinders our freedom to love. As we expand our vision and capacity to give and receive love, we will help bring to greater fullness the reign of God's love.

Your Crisis Is Your Crisis

There is no way to predict how people will respond to a crisis. Their history, culture, gender, and supports (or lack of them) exert influence, as do the impact of the initiating event and the intensity of suffering. For example, after a flood people face the clean-up: mud, foul odor, humidity and heat, efforts to save things of value, especially photos and other special items, working with insurance companies and government offices, and healing from loss and exhaustion. Sometimes the domino effect in a crisis brings added stress: a child is seriously injured; Mom needs to be with her in the hospital for weeks and months and loses her job, which cannot be held open for her any longer; the other children at home feel abandoned and neglected; the insurance coverage comes to an end.

When there is extreme suffering, escalated by the realization that people who have died are gone permanently and that life will never return to "normal," coping can be excruciating. It is a nightmare from which people wish they could wake up, but when they awaken, the painful dream continues into the day. How they make sense of the situation is crucial to moving beyond coping to healing. Often people's relationship with God becomes very important. God might be their strength and comfort. Sometimes God is questioned about God's care and reasons for causing or allowing the misfortune to occur. At times these perspectives are often experienced simultaneously, as is evident in the following event.

When John and Lisa's young son, Scott, died in a house fire, they agonized beyond anything they could imagine. John wept, feeling his heart was broken. And nothing could mend it. He also writhed in the pain of questions that brought no answers: Why? Why was my son taken from me? Why did he die such a painful death? And it isn't fair that he died so tragically! Why did he have to give up his life when it was just beginning? As he questioned, John also felt a trace of hope that someday he would understand why the disaster happened and why he and his family were subjected to this excruciating suffering. With understanding, some peace might be given him. His grief might be calmed.

Lisa also described her varying feelings. While trusting that God would see her and the rest of her family through and beyond the tragedy, anger at God nearly overwhelmed her. The questions of "why?" and "how?" loomed big for her as they did for John: Why didn't God intervene and spare Scott's life? Why was her family given the pain they were experiencing, pain no one could take from them? How could they go on when everywhere around the house there were reminders of Scott: his Teddy Bear, favorite CD that served as his bedtime story book, flannel pajamas covered with outer-space figures, and breakfast cereal that was his, mostly because no one else liked it? No one gave her satisfactory answers. Lisa received no indications that God heard her questions and expressions of pain and anger. However, she had to say them. She believed that God was open to such honesty; God's heart was big enough to hold her rage.

While feeling the traumatic effects of Scott's death and her anger, she also felt that God was with her. This feeling was hard to explain, and yet it was real. God was supporting her and her family through the people around her; she felt an inner strength she'd never experienced before. There were moments when she sensed God cared intimately for all of them. Gratitude for her belief that Scott was with God and other family members who had died gave her some peace. At times Lisa questioned how her pain and sorrow could be present along with a sense of occasional calm, emotions we normally do not imagine occurring simultaneously. She bowed to the mystery of it all, a mystery held by a God who she believed loved her no matter what she said and did, no matter what happened in her life.

A person grounded in Christian spirituality gains support to walk as a participant in the journey of Christ and in the adventures of the total Body of Christ living through people today. For example, someone told me about her friend, Josie, who believes she is participating in the dying and rising of Christ as she surrenders to the pain of psychotherapy during which she is dealing with her childhood experiences of sexual abuse. At times she feels she has lived quite well in denial during the first thirty-five years of her life, and she asks herself why she should go through what it will take to gain freedom. The answer to her question is not an easy one.

One dynamic of freedom Josie desperately wants is to be able to accept love. The abuse inflicted on her was done under the guise of love, so her ability to accept love as an adult has been seriously damaged. Her faith in Christ and his power to heal and bring her freedom through her suffering help keep her resolute to continue walking toward life. Josie carries a conviction that as she heals, she will enable others to heal from abuse, whether it is through her presence or service of ministry. These beliefs that are being massaged deeply into her heart are helping her to walk more willingly into the work of the dying she is being asked to do. Through her dying, she is rising to a fuller living of the life of Christ.

We return to the conviction that each person's crisis needs to be respected as personal and unique to the situation. Sometimes, usually after the stress has subsided, we second guess ourselves and discredit the role the experience has played in our life. It can seem trivial and inconsequential. "It really wasn't so bad." Also, we compare ourselves to people who have or are undergoing suffering beyond what we can imagine. While some comparing can help us put our experience into perspective, it can also pose a danger of dishonoring our own experience and what God is doing in our life.

Most of our crises occur as a "normal" part of life. Ordinary life gives us challenges and lessons; some come suddenly and dramatically, others brew over an extended time. While we usually don't want extremely dramatic crises, we still often hold them as more significant than the mundane ups and downs of life. Humility calls us to accept what we are given and to open ourselves to its possibilities rather than worrying about its degree of trauma. What is is, and our responsibility is to stop, look, and listen and to take appropriate steps.

The Coming of the Dawn

People whose wisdom comes through the written word or presentations can become significant companions in our journey through a crisis. Wise guidance through critical times can also be found in reading and seminars. While browsing through the spirituality section of a bookstore or library we find sources that provide insights and suggestions from people who, actual or fictional, have walked a journey of suffering. In *Man's Search for Meaning*, Viktor Frankl tells of his days and struggles for survival in the Nazi death camps. Numerous works about Dorothy Day provide insight into her untiring work for social justice. Lily Owens, the fictional young girl in *The Secret Life of Bees*, shares with us her search for love and her care about the equality of African Americans. All of these people, together with Benedict of Nursia and his guide for living, give us words and examples that make them appropriate companions on our journey through crisis and the day-to-day encounters. Scripture texts can help root our trust in God's care and strength. Assurances such as the following can speak to a troubled heart:

> Jesus says, "Come to me, all you that are weary and are carrying heavy burdens, and I will give you rest" (Matt 11:28). Rest might not come readily, but Jesus' compassion and care bring peace and encouragement in turmoil.

> The psalmist portrays God as the Good Shepherd, who is our Good Shepherd:

The Lord is my shepherd, I shall not want.
He makes me lie down in green pastures;
he leads me beside still waters;
he restores my soul.
He leads me in right paths
for his name's sake.

Even though I walk through the darkest valley,
I fear no evil;
for you are with me;
your rod and your staff—
they comfort me. (Ps 23:1-4)

When I read some of the insights of Gerald May, who died in 2005 after a long illness, I found affirmation of my own and others' experiences. He describes the emergence out of the darkness of a crisis or "dark night" as the coming of the dawn in early morning. The light is muted rather than shining with the brightness of the sun at midday.[5] This description describes well my experience of second semester when a new day gradually began to dawn. I sensed more light slowly coming into my days. New classes gave me opportunities to open new relationships. I felt accepted and was not defending myself against antagonists. My creativity began to return as I planned and conducted class activities. Rather than feeling doubt and failure about my teaching, I became confirmed in my vocation as a teacher and facilitator of learning. I was amazed at how often I felt gratitude when something happened that I judged to be a positive indicator that my path had shifted. I prayed inner litanies of thankfulness for God's support and for those who helped me walk through the first semester.

May also talks about the simultaneous dynamic of walking in the increasing light while making our way in some degree of darkness.[6] My coming into the light was not instantaneous; it came gradually. I could not force the light to come. Its arrival stood outside my control. May echoes my experience when he notes one of the gifts of the dawn: "an awakening to a deepening realization of who we really are in and with God and the world, and of what has been going on within us in the night. Always, and most important, the dawn is an awakening in love."[7] I came to realize that throughout my fall semester I had yearned to return to my usual self. In the end, I discovered I had become a new self. And this self was bigger in perspective and able to hold people in deeper care than before. My dawn was an "awakening in love" for myself and others and for my relationship with God. Living in the confusion and vulnerability gave me insight and compassion to and for others. I became aware of some of the gifts I had been given through not knowing, feeling insecure in my attempted usual ways of acting, and my customary understandings of life and its meaning.

The image of the dawn breaking into the night is renewed for me every day during Morning Prayer when my monastic community prays this verse that is part of Zechariah's prophecy at the time of the circumcision and naming of his and Elizabeth's son, John the Baptist:

> "By the tender mercy of our God,
>   the dawn from on high will break upon us,
> to give light to those who sit in darkness and in the shadow
>   of death,
>   to guide our feet into the way of peace." (Luke 1:78-79)

These words speak not only of my journey but also of those of others, whether or not we are in crisis. We hope for the rising of the morning sun and the coming of the compassion of God through the graced encounters in our day. Then we will be given light, joy, life, and love. The promise of light dawning also gives me hope for our global community that is in travail. Natural disasters, political tragedies, and economic crises constantly threaten our personal and global stability and existence. They challenge my faith and expectations for blessings of mercy and justice to all. The Body of Christ is struggling for life. The Giver of Life gives me hope every morning.

Crisis Miles; Daily Steps

As we begin to traverse any crisis, the end seems impossible or at least to be far away. This distance is a gift; it gives us the time needed for the work of transformation to occur. Within the miles of this journey, we stumble and walk through many events. Though not dramatic, they will be the stepping stones through the crisis. At times we will be amazed at how seemingly incidental encounters will stand out from the background so we can greet them as special and as offerings of support and signs of care from people and God.

While moving through a crisis, it is crucial that we engage in tasks that will ground us and bring us physically into our usual time and space. Some of my friends have found that getting their hands into the soil while gardening has been healing for them. Others make sure they clean, wash dishes, mow the grass, and talk with family and friends. One friend watches videos of comedies. She says her endorphins love them, and she feels better. For some, going to concerts and places of beauty (art museums, scenic landscapes) brings solace and healing. A co-worker continues her fishing outings; she moves into the care of friends and solitude in the boat and on the water. For some, daily meditation and prayer serve as anchoring points that renew their perspective and trust in God, even though they do not receive the answers they seek.

While our engagement with the stuff of daily life helps us take one step at a time, these activities are more supportive than they might otherwise have been when done within a context of meaning that helps give us purpose. This is particularly true when the context is rooted in a tradition of transcendent values and goals. I found that Jonathan Rosen's words were accurate for me as I drew from my Christian faith: "Tradition is kind of like the railing of the bridge. The bridge is still narrow and it's still suspended over darkness. But there's something to hold onto that lots of other people have held onto."[8] I walk with a strong railing of my faith tradition and spirituality. When it wobbles for me, I try to hold onto it more firmly for balance, and at times I call on God and my companions to help steady it. Sometimes I look into the darkness below and sometimes I don't have the courage to do so. Regardless of my reaction, I am called to keep on moving. There is land—new land—on the other side.

When I look around me, there are many people on the bridge. I'm not the only one moving to the other side over and through darkness, so there is no room for self-pity. I'm amazed that supporting others on their tenuous adventure helps to stabilize me. I expend my energy, otherwise bound in fear and self-preservation, for a purpose that brings life. I also discover that our precarious situation urges me to reach out for support from people who are with me or who have walked a little ahead of me and who can point out a few steps that might be helpful.

Our messy and sometimes misguided steps through a crisis offer possibilities for us to groan with all creation as we await and work for the fullness of transformation (Rom 8:22-25). Christ groans with and through us. The Spirit guides and nurtures us to full fruition of the life begun in all of us. Together we await the dawn to break upon us. God's compassion and commitment to life will eventually bring all into fullness. In the meantime, we "hope for what we do not see" and "we wait for it with patience" (Rom 8:25).

Chapter 7

Living in a Sacred Place: Living Contemplatively

Even though "the acquisition of a heart is a life-long process"
it is what I deeply desire and I believe that if I desire it I
shall find nurture and support in many ways: through other
people, through prayer and study, through the circumstances
of my life. But above all it will be in ways that I probably am
unaware of and certainly do not understand—the
inexhaustible mystery of God at work on me, the shaping,
moulding, enlarging of a heart that will become increasingly
permeable to God as my journey unfolds.[1]

Living in a Sacred Place

Sister Marold lives in a tent that, for her, is a holy place. She calls it her meeting tent with God. She usually is referring to her bedroom when she talks about her meeting tent. However, as I have come to know Sister Marold, I realize that the whole world is a meeting tent where she walks, talks, and lives with God. The world is a temple, a sacred place where any event can provide an opportunity to meet and respond to God.

When I conversed with Sister Marold recently about her living in God's tent, she spontaneously prayed a litany of thanks, the kind she prays every day as she moves from her room, down an elevator from fourth floor, and along a short sidewalk to chapel for Morning Prayer.

Thank you God, for the wonderful night of rest.
Thank you for the wonder of my being which you knit so
          marvelously
   in my mother's womb.
Thank you for the events that lie ahead of me: the elevator
working,
   the shiver that awakens my body as I step outdoors, the
breakfast
          that awaits me,
   the conversation with the sisters working around me later
today.
Thank you for my mended heart [following serious by-pass
          surgery].
Please God, find a place in it and help me see you in all that
          happens today
   and in everyone I meet
      —in the dining room
      —when I'm doing my quilling.
I put all in your hands.
Thank you for my mom whose picture is on my desk.
   She is smiling and I smile back. Sometimes a tear plops
down
      my cheek . . .
   but off we go, God, Mom and me.[2]

For Sister Marold the entire world is a temple where all the people, things, and events speak to her of God's lavish generosity, manifested event by event and permeating every encounter. In this holy place God cares for her and the rest of creation. Her responses highlight wonder and gratitude. The members of my monastic community know her as the one who sings her praise with tunes of her own composing at the spur of the moment.

Sister Marold helps to answer my question of younger years when I first learned that St. Benedict tells us to pray constantly (RB 4:56; cf. 1 Thess 5:17): How can I do it? She shows me this type of prayer is a way of life; it depends on how we look at and respond to everyday events. Her life is a prayer. She and God, her companion, walk through days together. She also helps me understand St. Benedict's wisdom when he points out that our living the way of Christ and growing in our relationship with God is narrow at first but then gets easier, even making our hearts overflow with the delight of love that is beyond expression (RB Prol 48-49).

Sister Marold has experienced painful situations in her life and most recently has made her way through grieving the death of her beloved brother and her own serious health issues. Her life journey has been marked with trials. As she has become older, her worries, losses, and physical pain have increased. I see a paradox: while life sometimes is daunting for Sister Marold, she knows from within that she and God are intimate friends. Within her heart, a heart formed and expanded over many years, everything comes together, and Sister Marold runs with the joy of her relationship with God. In pain, she hopes, even though she falters at times; in fear, she moves to courage and dependence on God and those helping her; in doubt about her future, she struggles to trust that God will be there with and for her.

A Disciple Who Practices

Sister Marold, age ninety-three, exhibits the expansion of heart that is possible when we let life touch us over and over. She demonstrates that through daily events our perceptions open to broader and more embracing dimensions. These same events can mold our hearts to love more habitually through expressions such as patience, courage, lightheartedness, empathy, willingness to speak our truth, and joy. Our everyday experiences ground our feet on the earth where life is occurring.

As happens when we learn a skill, we need to practice, an activity that often is boring and tedious. Repeatedly we will encounter situations in which we will be given opportunities to improve our skills to live as disciples of Christ. At times we will fail; we try again next time. I recall the many times as a child I skipped practicing the assigned scales as part of my learning to play the piano. Somehow I thought the teacher wouldn't notice. I do not think she would be surprised today to discover that I am not skilled in playing the piano. However, I have learned the value of practice in other realms of my life. For instance, practice through actions such as listening, journaling, and developing relationships is essential for learning how to live as a person in God's world.

To live mindfully and to develop the vision and qualities of Christ usually require many years. Through baptism we have been drawn into the life of God. Over time, we learn through our communities, study, reflection, and prayer what types of responses support God's vision for the good of all the members of the Body of Christ. Comfort, security, and self-interest then move down from the top of our agenda. Instead, forgiveness of others and ourselves, joy, and gratitude mark our lives. God calls us to put effort into the quality and results of our work. This way of working makes us cocreators with God in the ongoing development of creation in which we are called to participate. Facing issues such as fear and shame is part of our own healing and ongoing creation. We learn that it is an illusion that monotony and dryness in our lives, especially in our prayer, are of little value. Sometimes we even laugh at the unlikely places God dwells and considers holy.

We hold to the conviction that we are seeking God and are both finding and being found in the search. Our relationship with God in love pulls us to serve and collaborate with the people in our immediate situations and in the broader community. Involvement in working for social consciousness and responsibility becomes a normal part of our lives.[3] Movements such as these occur within the realm of daily life. They are the daily musical scales that need to be practiced, each time expanding our hearts to be able to love more unconditionally in all situations. Our practicing is an asceticism of daily life, an athletic activity that builds strength and expands our heart and lung capacity. This type of exercise will gradually form our hearts into gospel hearts.

Many people come to a time in their lives when they need glasses to be able to see clearly. Furthermore, as life goes on, the need for change reoccurs, sometimes with increased frequency or major correction such as a lens implant. Events of our daily lives nudge us into adjustments that challenge us to let go of our constrictive judgments and feelings so we can open to seeing in a new way. Developmental stages of life such as adolescence, midlife, and senior elders draw us into new perceptions. They move us through life tasks that are accomplished through the stuff of our lives, current and past and with an eye to the future.

College graduates who are moving into their first professional work face challenges to their identity and competence as they enter an arena of competition and new expectations. They may also feel lonely without their easy access to friends and social life on their college campus. In turn, parents move into shifting life patterns, work aspirations, and relationships when their children leave home to establish their lives elsewhere. Some experience relief and opening to aspirations they have had for themselves; for others, it is loneliness and loss of purpose.

Regardless of the developmental tasks, all are called to new possibilities that require the wisdom gained from past experiences and practice. They also can benefit by walking with others who have walked the journey a few steps ahead of them or with companions asking the same questions and tentatively putting a foot forward on a new path.

More Practice

In addition to the practice we exercise in the unpredictable and given encounters of life—the people, situations, and our own responses—various tools can support our life journey. Although I have noted several throughout the chapters of this book, I will highlight two of them here: prayerful reading (*lectio divina*) and "time out." I have found these practices to be basic in helping me develop and live within a context of significant meaning. For example, regular times of *lectio divina* based on Jesus Christ and his mission keep me grounded in my call to seek and meet God in my daily life. The gospels give me a vision of the reign of God's love. My world is nourished by the same kinds of touches Christ brought to his time and place. When I am discouraged because I am not making much progress in learning to live the gospel or because I am drawing too much on my own efforts, a psalm or other biblical text often pulls me back to center.

> Create in me a clean heart, O God,
>   and put a new and right spirit within me. . . .
> Restore me to the joy of your salvation,
>   and sustain in me a willing spirit. (Ps 51:10, 12)

The Scripture texts remind me that God takes the initiative and God sustains.

The Word of God continues to come into our midst and be revealed. With this conviction, we can look to the revelations of God's communications that come through our daily lives. To help us listen, praying our experiences—practicing "*lectio* of life"—is an important form of prayer.[4] When I reflect on a conflict, whether internal or in relationship with another, and bring that conflict into a conversation with God, I may see and accept responsibility for my part in creating it. I might hear an invitation to forgive the other person and myself; I might be drawn to talk with her as a step of resolving the issue. Insights into myself open me to some of my growing edges and to opportunities where God has graced me in the relationship. At times I find words through a story, prayer, letter, or person in Scripture from which I draw wisdom. As the practice of *lectio* of life has become one of my forms of prayer, I have grown in awareness that I am living my sacred history and am contributing to the transformation of the broader world community—person by person, day by day.

Everyday activities and people become automatic and unimpressive, and I often feel their constancy and pressure. I find it helpful to step out from my normal situations and interactions for a while. Consciously creating a pause in my life, in my day, in the mundane can allow for new listening, reevaluation, and recommitment to principles that guide me. This stepping out can be a short stroll across campus, a half-hour walk in the woods, a drive home without conversation or radio communication, or twenty minutes of yoga. If brief pauses are important, longer pauses usually can bring expanded value.

In my monastic community we participate annually in a five-day retreat in which we practice much silence and often listen to reflections based on some dynamics of spiritual life given by a presenter. Hence, we open to renewed rooting and fresh perspectives that can feed us and support our commitment to live monastic life in this community. We receive no guarantee regarding the effects of the retreat, but we show up so we are present for whatever the Spirit gives us. I have also noticed that praying and being silent together unify us in ways not possible through conversation. Perhaps I am sensing that together we are with God and each other in God's meeting tent.

Anne Morrow Lindbergh took me to the ocean many years ago through her book, *Gift from the Sea*.[5] She describes her retreat experience in a simple cabin at the ocean through her reflection on seashells, each symbolizing a phase in her life. For about fifteen years, I read the book annually to renew my inspiration. At times I noticed that I was edging out of one phase of life and into another.

As Morrow Lindbergh leaves the retreat she notes that the basic substance of life is found in the "small circle of the home," people, the here and now in all its liveliness. She states with renewed conviction, "We may neglect these elements, but we cannot dispense with them." I agree with her. A retreat helps us receive a new look at the daily elements of home; we get to see new perspectives. We also move into deeper understandings and solutions of challenges. Sometimes I think the situation has changed when, in fact, it is I who has changed. In addition, Morrow Lindbergh points out that we can then also affect other situations: "When we start at the center of ourselves, we discover something worthwhile extending toward the periphery of the circle. We find again some of the joy in the now, some of the peace in the here, some of the love in me and thee which go to make up the kingdom of heaven on earth." Withdrawing for a time each day, several times a week, or a longer time, helps us return to and open the "center of ourselves" in our daily lives, for the sake of our own lives and those of others.

St. Benedict's Vision: All in a Ray of Light

St. Benedict saw life as a journey. His verbs, such as running, walking, hastening, indicate the dynamism of a lifelong process. He is shown in *The Life and Miracles of St. Benedict* by Gregory the Great as wrestling with his vocation as a hermit and as a leader of monasteries.[6] He gradually moves into a deeper and deeper relationship with God and exercises many of the attitudes and powers of Christ. Near the end of his life he experienced a wonder that expressed the wisdom into which he had grown through a lifetime of practice, patience, and remaining focused on his commitment to God.

The event precedes the final phase of Benedict's journey home where he would meet God in fullness. Gregory describes a vision of St. Benedict in which he sees the entire world gathered up in a ray of light. Benedict was standing at his window during the middle of the night; he was watching and praying. Gregory depicts the scene: Suddenly Benedict saw a "flood of light shining down from above more brilliant than the sun, and with it every trace of darkness cleared away. . . . According to his own description, the whole world was gathered up before his eyes in what appeared to be a single ray of light."

Peter, to whom Gregory is telling the story, exclaims: "What an astounding miracle!" He also questions how a person can see the entire universe in one glance. Gregory explains:

> All creation is bound to appear small to a soul that sees the Creator. Once it beholds a little of His light, it finds all creatures

small indeed. The light of holy contemplation enlarges and expands the mind in God until it stands above the world. In fact, the soul that sees Him rises even above itself, and as it is drawn upward in His light all its inner powers unfold. Then, when it looks down from above, it sees how small everything really is that was beyond its grasp before. . . . I do not mean that heaven and earth grew small, but that his spirit was enlarged. Absorbed as he was in God, it was now easy for him to see all that lay beneath God. In the light outside that was shining before his eyes, there was a brightness which reached into his mind and lifted his spirit heavenward, showing him the insignificance of all that lies below.

On first reading, this episode could discredit the significance we have been reflecting on in regard to the sacredness of persons, things, places, and events in our daily lives. All is insignificant in comparison with God. Giving the account a second look, we receive a glimpse of Benedict's contemplative vision. All is seen in its proper relationship to God; all is good while not being the final goal of our thirsting and hungering. All is encompassed in the light of God's radiance. We discover that the issue is more our attitude toward these realities than the created beings themselves. We are the ones who make them self-serving in our lives. We give them disproportionate value.

When we consider these realities with an enlarged spirit as Christ and St. Benedict did, we, too, stand in a right relationship with them—honoring them in their own right without possessing them only as means to our satisfaction. If this stance were not true, how could we pray some of the psalms that acknowledge the wonders of created things and draw them into the praise of God: rain, grass, plants, fodder, wheat, and wind in Psalm 147; sea monsters, fire and hail, snow and mist, mountains, orchards, cedars, animals, and birds in Psalm 148. In Psalm 139 we are given a glimpse of God's personal and sensitive love for us: God knits us together and knows us in the womb, knows parts of us we ourselves do not know. This psalm also refers to the wonder that we are and praises all God's works as wonders. This same theme of wonder and the goodness of all God created is conveyed in the creation story in Genesis 1. I imagine that whenever God looks at creation, God ecstatically exclaims, "How good it all is! It is all sacred!"

Everyday Mysticism

Karl Rahner, SJ, put contemporary words on Gregory's interpretation of St. Benedict's vision and perspective on daily life. He writes about the "mysticism of everyday life" where we are given a personal experience of God, even though it does not seem dramatic.[7] Rahner relates to a mysticism that is down to earth. He gives us the message that "a genuine Christian who lives the mysticism of daily life possesses the bold, but often hidden confidence that ordinary daily life is the stuff of authentic life and real Christianity."[8] This "stuff" is comprised of all experiences, regardless of whether we label them as joyful, sad, challenging, boring, ecstatic, painful, gray, or bright.[9] Building on Rahner's view, Eagan says: "In fact, we weave the fabric of our eternal lives out of our humdrum days."[10]

All our everyday encounters offer possibilities for the expansion of our heart, for a deepening of our transformation. At times we are given glances of the richness of our existence. For instance, a newborn infant evokes wonder. God is praised, explicitly or implicitly. The sisters of my monastery walk delightfully through the summer months in awe as they plant their hobby gardens, announce the first sprouting and beginning signs of fruit, and harvest what God has given them. They also know devastation emotionally when a hail storm destroys the plants or the nearby deer think it is their garden, too, and munch their way through it at night. A friend struggled through three years of her dad's deteriorating health that ended in death; as exhausted and frustrated as she became, she saw something in his life that she wanted to support and care for. I sensed she found the goodness of God in him, even when he was cranky and demeaning of her. On days when I recognize I have failed in receiving a colleague hospitably, I feel the need to open to Christ's healing; I ask for help. The failure makes me available to grace. And I get to start again; I can always begin over.

A letter from Sophia, one of my former students who is serving in Ghana through the Peace Corps, pulls my imagination to a country and people that are very different from mine. I am grateful for the success of some of the new farming efforts—efforts that were given through the humdrum of daily life—and for Sophia, who is willing to give two years of her life to such service. Situations such as these live out of the creative energy of God and sweep us into the same energy and purpose. The heart of God opens to us. Our hearts expand and open to all creation.

Eagan continues his discussion of Rahner's thought: "This mysticism of everyday life encompasses even the most humble aspects of our daily routine, such as our working, sleeping, eating, drinking, laughing, seeing, sitting, and getting about."[11] In situations such as these, grace is experienced. Rahner reflects: "Grace has its history in man's day-to-day existence with its splendors and failures and is *actually experienced there.*"[12] Reflections with people such as Rahner and St. Benedict, who serve as a basis of *lectio divina*, open us to the possibility of living as a mystic in everyday life.[13] Thus, as we live with a sacramental view of life, trusting that any encounter can serve as a meeting of God and as an opportunity to respond, we are living contemplatively, as a mystic.

Missed Opportunities

Sometimes it helps us to see the contrast between mindful living and openness to encounters. Recently I attended a performance of one of my favorite plays, *Our Town.*[14] Having seen it several times before, I observed details I had not seen or heard previously. I noted especially the minimal attention and communication that occurs throughout people's lives. Family members exchange words but seldom stop what they are doing to give their presence through eye contact and responding to the feelings of the speaker. Daily life moves at a hurried pace that does not easily allow for such human expressions. People perform the service daily life calls for, but rarely do they give emotional care with the action. They also get caught up in the ordinariness of the people and activities of their lives. This day-to-day ordinariness holds them in a mundane routine that enables them to move through their activities without much engagement beyond surface exchanges within meetings of each other. Their usual patterns confine them in relationships and interactions that do not call for much reflection and authentic presence.

Toward the end of the play one of the characters, Emily, dies during the birth of her second child. She enters the graveyard, where she finds other deceased townspeople. This place has not yet become her new home. She longs to return to Grover's Corners for one more look at her earthly world.

The stage manager of the play consents to let Emily return to her hometown and family to visit on an ordinary day. She moves among familiar people without being seen. After all, having died, she now is a spirit. Emily's vantage point is radically different from that of her family as they go about their daily lives. In a pained plea she begs her mother to look at her. As was true when Emily talked with her mother while she was alive, there is no eye contact or engagement with her now.

As Emily ends her visit to her family, amid sobs she tells the stage manager who has accompanied her that she cannot go on. She agonizes about a life that moves so quickly that people who care about each other miss opportunities to just look at each other. She realizes that much goes on that people do not notice.

Before leaving to return to her grave, Emily says good-bye to her hometown—people in her family and details she now sees and hears, perhaps for the first time: the sounds of clocks, her mother's sunflowers, food she was used to eating, baths, and daily actions such as sleeping and waking. Her good-bye expresses a new awareness, wonder, and appreciation for human experience and the journeys people walk. Deceased and leaving to return to her grave, Emily is now awake to the simple wonders around her. She is conscious, and in this new awareness, she is alive.

Emily's plea for her mother to look at her echoes deep in our own hearts. Sometimes we are aware of it; sometimes it is numbed by our own and others' lack of attention to our concerns. We also experience the challenges of breaking out of our usual perceptions, the fast pace of life, and distractions that take us in many directions. Emily challenges us with questions: Do we need the threat that people, things, and activities of our daily life will be taken away before we notice and value them? What will help open us to give and receive presence and care from ourselves and others?

Perhaps Emily's experience can sound an alarm that will bring us out of the stupor of inattentive movement through our days. As a result, more of our everyday encounters will become blessings rather than lie dormant as missed opportunities. These blessings will release compassion, wonder, respect, and care for all beings. Thus we expand the possibilities for God's vision to be realized: that love becomes the foundation and spirit of all our encounters with people, things, and the rest of creation.

We Continue to Run with an Expanding Heart

We are called to advance on our journey, whether the pace be walking, stumbling, or running, with an expanding heart that receives and gives love. As we step into the future of the next few moments, weeks, and years, the contemporary psalmist, John O'Donohue, prays a blessing for us:

> May you awaken to the mystery of being here and enter
> the quiet immensity of your own presence.
> May you have peace and joy in the temple of your senses.
> May you receive great encouragement when new frontiers
> beckon.
> May you respond to the call of your gift and find the
> courage to follow its path. . . .

May your outer dignity mirror an inner dignity of soul.
May you take time to celebrate the quiet miracles that
    seek no attention.
May you be consoled in the secret symmetry of your soul.
May you experience each day as a sacred gift woven
    around the heart of wonder.[15]

May our heart of wonder join God's wonder as we live God's affirmation: "How good it all is! It is all sacred!"

Notes

Preface, pages xv–xvii

1. *Rule of Benedict 1980*, ed. Timothy Fry (Collegeville, MN: Liturgical Press, 1982). Future references to the Rule of Benedict will be from this edition. St. Benedict uses the term "monks" to refer to members of male monasteries. In this contemporary time the term "monastic" is being used to refer to men and women who live according to the Rule of Benedict. I will use this term when talking about present-day men and women followers of the Rule of Benedict.

2. *St. Benedict's Rule for Monasteries*, trans. Leonard J. Boyle. (Collegeville, MN: Liturgical Press, 1948), 5. The text referring to hearts expanding is basic to one of the underlying metaphors of this book. Doyle translates Prologue 49 as follows: "For as we advance in the religious life and in faith, our hearts expand and we run the way of God's commandments with unspeakable sweetness of love."

3. J. Matt Hershel, *Walking Humbly with God: The Life and Writings of Rabbi Hershel Jonah Matt*, ed. Daniel C. Matt (Hoboken, NJ: KTAV Publishing House, 1993), 147; originally in Hershel J. Matt, "Miracle and *Berakhah*: How Shall We Approach the Miracles of the Bible?" *Synagogue School* 22, no.3 (Spring 1964): 6–13.

4. Ibid.

Chapter 1, pages 1–11

1. Abraham Joshua Heschel, *Man Is Not Alone* (New York: Harper and Row, 1951), 5.

2. Esther de Waal, *Seeking God: The Way of St. Benedict* (Collegeville, MN: Liturgical Press, 1984), 30–31. See de Waal's comments regarding

the focus of the *Rule of Benedict* and its purpose of serving to help ordinary people live lives of "quite extraordinary value" as they focus on Christ as individuals and as a community.

3. Peter Mayer, "Everything Is Holy Now," in *Million Year Mind* (Atlanta, GA: Peppermint Records and Tapes, 2000). The phrase, "everything is holy," serves as the basis of the title of a song by Peter Mayer. In it he celebrates the sacredness of all creation. He also reminds us that wonders (miracles) still happen today in the midst of our daily lives.

4. Annie Dillard, *Pilgrim at Tinker Creek* (New York: Bantam Books, 1984), 16.

5. Ibid.

6. Gerard Manley Hopkins, SJ, *The Works of Gerard Manley Hopkins*, ed. Catherine Phillips (New York: Oxford University Press, 1995), 26.

7. Sylvia Sultenfuss, "Out of the Ordinary" (unpublished poem).

8. Heschel, *Man Is Not Alone*, 5.

9. Peter Fransen, *The New Life of Grace* (New York: Seabury Press, 1969), 331–332.

Chapter 2, pages 12–26

1. Barry Lopez, "In Little Things I Find the Cosmos," *Wildlife*, 2, no. 2 (February-March, 1973): 42.

2. Gail Godwin, *Evensong* (New York: Ballantine Books, 1999), 12. Godwin says: "Something's one's vocation if it keeps making more of you."

3. Paul Ricoeur, *The Philosophy of Paul Ricoeur: An Anthology of His Work*, trans. Charles E. Reagan and David Stewart (Boston: Beacon Press, 1978), 241–242. See also, John Taylor, *The Go-Between God: The Holy Spirit and the Christian Mission* (New York: Oxford University Press, 1972), 3–24. Taylor discusses moments of ordinary life that catch or demand our attention as "annunciations" in which the seer recognizes God and God sees the person.

4. Ibid.

5. Ibid., 239. A similar perspective is given by Paul van Buren: "The decisive point to be made is that some men are *struck* by the ordinary, whereas most find it merely ordinary. . . . Seeing the ordinary as extraordinary, as a cause for wonder, is no more and no less in need of justifica-

tion than seeing the ordinary as ordinary and as something to be taken for granted" (*Theological Explorations* [SCM Press, 1968], 170–71), quoted in John Taylor, *The Go-Between God: The Holy Spirit and the Christian Mission* (New York: Oxford University Press, 1979), 12.

6. Mary Wolf, "Thin Place," http://justus.anglican.org/sabbath-blessings/1999/sb31.html. Mary Anthony Wagner, OSB, explores the topic of "thin spots" from the perspective of Native Americans in *The Sacred World of the Christian: Sensed in Faith* (Collegeville, MN: Liturgical Press, 1993), 28, 30, 35, 86, 101, 108. For further discussion of "thin times," especially through the use of ritual, see Wagner, part 1, "Another World: Its Myths and Rituals," 11–36.

7. Wolf, "Thin Place."

8. John Miriam Jones, SC, quoted in Susan Hines-Brigger, "Irish Journey into Celtic Spirituality," http://www.americancatholic.org/Messenger/Mar2001/feature1.asp.

9. Virginia Woolf, *Moments of Being: Unpublished Autobiographical Writings*, ed. Jeanne Schulkind (New York: Harcourt, Brace and Jovanovich, 1996), 72. Further use of the phrases "cotton wool" and "cotton wool of daily life" are taken from this source.

10. For a discussion about the benefits of living as a conscious adult, see Sylvia Sultenfuss, "Designing and Sustaining the Spiritually Conscious Adult," in *The Joy of Adulthood: A Crash Course in Designing the Life You Want* (Atlanta: Palladium Productions, 2004), 93–119.

11. Czeslaw Milosz, "Beyond My Strength," in *Road-side Dog*, trans. Czeslaw Milosz and Robert Hass (New York: Farrar, Straus and Giroux, 1998), 104.

12. Elisabeth Frink, "Walking Madonna," Salisbury Cathedral, England. Photographed by Michael Blackman, Camerawork, Lake, Salisbury. Published by Pitkin Pictorials Ltd., Healey House, Dandover, Hants. Further use of parts of this phrase is from the words on the postcard.

13. Benedict of Nursia, *St. Benedict's Rule for Monasteries*, trans. Leonard Doyle (Collegeville, MN: Liturgical Press, 1948), 5. Doyle reads: "For as we advance in the religious life and in faith, our hearts expand and we run the way of God's commandments with unspeakable sweetness of love." In contrast, RB 80 translates Prologue 49: "our hearts overflowing with the inexpressible delight of love."

14. Marie Biddle, SJ, photographer of the "Walking Madonna" and woman in the background.

Chapter 3, pages 27–44

1. Demetrius Dumm, OSB, "Benedictine Hospitality," *Benedictines* 35, no. 2 (Fall-Winter, 1980): 64–75.

2. Ibid., 65.

3. Ibid., 68.

4. For an exploration of hospitality and stewardship from a biblical perspective, see Monika Hellwig, *Guests of God: Stewards of Divine Creation* (New York: Paulist Press, 1999), 7.

5. Gunilla Norris, "Dusting," in *Being Home: A Book of Meditations* (New York: Bell Tower, 1991), 25–26. The quoted sections of "Dusting" are taken from pages 25–26.

6. C.B. Hackworth and Andrew Young, *Rwanda Rising* (Atlanta: Good Works Productions, 2006), video recording.

7. Mary Reuter, OSB, "Time on our Hands, Time in Our Hearts," *Review for Religious* 45, no.2 (March-April, 1986): 256. The article gives a fuller discussion of a contemplative attitude toward time, 256–265.

8. Zalman Schachter, quoted in "Ministry of Money: Exploring Money and Spirituality" (September-October, 2001): 5, http://www.ministry ofmoney.org/PDFs/MoM%20Newltr%20129.pdf.

9. For a discussion of time from the perspective of the Scriptures, keeping the Sabbath, and living in sabbath time throughout the week, see Dorothy Bass, *Receiving the Day: Christian Practices for Opening the Gift of Time* (San Francisco: Jossey-Bass, 2000).

Chapter 4, pages 45–60

1. Scott Russell Sanders, "A Private History of Awe," *Orion Magazine* (January, 2003): 58. Further references to Sanders are taken from this source.

2. Barbara Myerhoff , *Number Our Days* (New York: Simon and Schuster, Touchstone Edition, 1980), 188.

3. Ibid.

4. Ibid., 189.

5. Yaffa Eliach , "Responses to Silence: The Tower of Life at the Holocaust Museum," Jay Phillips Lecture, College of Saint Benedict/Saint John's University, November 16, 1998. For further reading related to Eliach's experience, see her book, *There Once Was a World: A Nine-Hundred-Year*

Chronicle of the Shtetl of Eishyshok (Boston: Little, Brown and Company, 1998).

6. Rachel Remen, *My Grandfather's Blessings: Stories, Strength, and Belonging* (New York: Riverhead Books, 2000), 17.

7. Ibid.

8. Thich Nhat Hanh, paraphrased in Jon Frandsen, "Buddhist Monk Cultivates Mindfulness with Lectures, Encourages People to Live Life in Present," *St. Cloud Times* (January 4, 1998): 1B. See also Thich Nhat Hanh, *The Miracle of Mindfulness* (Boston: Beacon Press, 1976). Hanh, a Buddhist monk, offers perspectives on living mindfully with an awareness of what we are doing, such as eating, smelling, and touching.

9. Thich Nhat Hanh, in Frandsen, "Buddhist Monk Cultivates Mindfulness," 1B.

Chapter 5, pages 61–75

1. Demetrius Dumm, OSB, Retreat at Saint Benedict's Monastery, St. Joseph, MN, 1972.

2. See Esther de Waal, *Seeking God: The Way of St. Benedict* (Collegeville, MN: Liturgical Press, 1984), chapter 4. De Waal provides an insightful discussion of stability. Speaking of the tendency to avoid the here and now, she says: "Without stability . . . I may well end up flitting from one to the other until I have collected a ragbag for myself of well-intentioned but half-thought-out-ideals based on a confused and superficial amalgam of some of the more attractive elements in each. The danger then of course is that I too become confused and superficial" (56–57). De Waal also quotes Metropolitan Anthony Bloom regarding our stability and God's presence:

What is it then to be stable? . . . You will find stability at the moment when you discover that God is everywhere, that you do not need to seek Him elsewhere, that He is here, and if you do not find Him here, it is useless to go and search for Him elsewhere because it is not Him that is absent from us, it is we who are absent from Him. . . . It is only at the moment that you recognize this that you can truly find the fullness of the present in every situation and every place, that you will be able to say: "So then I shall stay where I am." (quoted in de Waal, 65)

3. Roger O. Hirson, *Pippin*, lyrics by Stephen Schwartz (New York: The Hearst Corporation, 1975).

4. Ibid., 98.

5. Augustine of Hippo, *The Confessions of St. Augustine*, trans. John K. Ryan (Garden City, NY: Doubleday and Company, 1960), 43). The reader is also referred to Ronald Rolheiser, *The Holy Longing: The Search for a Christian Spirituality* (New York: Random House, 1999), chapter 1. Rolheiser discusses a universal dis-ease that keeps humans dissatisfied and searching, searching ultimately for God.

6. Teresa of Avila, quoted in Ronald Rolheiser, the *Holy Longing*, 73.

> *Christ has no body now on earth but yours,*
> *no hands but yours,*
> *no feet but yours.*
> *Yours are the eyes through which*
> *Christ's compassion must look out on the world.*
> *Yours are the feet with which*
> *He is to go about doing good.*
> *Yours are the hands with which*
> *He is to bless us now.*

Chapter 6, pages 76–92

1. William Bridges, *Transitions: Making Sense of Life's Changes* (Reading, MA: Addison-Wesley, 1980), 96–98. See also Walter Brueggemann, "Letting Experience Touch the Psalter," in *Praying the Psalms* (Winona, MN: Saint Mary's Press, 1982), 15–25. Brueggemann discusses life experiences and the psalms from the perspective of orientation, disorientation, and reorientation.

2. Bridges, *Transitions*, 101.

3. Ibid., 102–104.

4. Ibid., 92–96.

5. Gerald May, *The Dark Night of the Soul: A Psychiatrist Explores the Connection Between Darkness and Spiritual Growth* (San Francisco: HarperCollins, 2004), 181. May bases his discussion on the "The Dark Night" by John of the Cross.

6. Ibid.

7. Ibid., 182. May quotes John of the Cross, "The Spiritual Canticle," in *The Collected Works of St. John of the Cross*, trans. K. Kavanaugh and O. Rodriguez (Washington, DC: Institute of Carmelite Studies, 1991), commentary on stanzas 14–15.

8. Jonathan Rosen, *Joy Comes in the Morning* (New York: Farrar, Straus and Giroux, 2004), 134.

Chapter 7, pages 93–106

1. Esther de Waal, *Seeking Life: The Baptismal Invitation of the Rule of St. Benedict* (Collegeville, MN: Liturgical Press, 2009), 88.

2. Marold Kornovich, OSB. Unpublished prayer, 2008. Sister Marold is a member of Saint Benedict's Monastery, St. Joseph, MN.

3. See Unites States Conference of Catholic Bishops, "Catholic Social Teaching and Principles," http://www.usccb.org/sdwp/catholicteaching-principles.shtml. These teachings articulate some of the major themes in Catholic social teaching that are intended to guide people's daily and organizational actions. They are especially significant for influencing systemic transformation.

4. For further discussion and suggestions for praying experiences, see Joseph Schmidt, FSC, *Praying Our Experiences* (Ijamsville, MD: The Word Among Us Press, 2008).

5. Anne Morrow Lindbergh, *Gift from the Sea* (New York: Pantheon Books, 1955). Quotations from this book are from pages 127–128.

6. Gregory the Great, *The Life and Miracles of St. Benedict*, trans. Odo J. Zimmermann, OSB, and Benedict R. Avery, OSB (Collegeville, MN: Liturgical Press). Quotations from this text are from pages 71–73. See also Katherine Howard's *Praying with Benedict* (Winona, MN: Saint Mary's Press, 1996.) This book provides a discussion of *The Life and Miracles of St. Benedict* as an aid to prayer.

7. Karl Rahner, quoted in Harvey D. Egan, *Karl Rahner: Mystic of Everyday Life* (New York: Crossroad, 1998), 57.

8. Harvey D. Egan, *Karl Rahner: Mystic of Everyday Life*, 59. Egan notes that this statement is a constant theme in Rahner's *Biblical Homilies*, trans. Desmond Forristal and Richard Strachan (New York: Herder and Herder, 1966).

9. Ibid., 57.

10. Ibid. Egan references Rahner, "Eternity from Time," in *Theological Investigations* (19): 169–177.

11. Egan, *Karl Rahner: Mystic of Everyday Life*, 58.

12. Ibid., 59. Egan quotes Rahner, "On the Theology of Worship" in *Theological Investigations* (19): 147. The emphasis is Egan's.

13. For additional reading regarding Benedict's dynamic and mystical view of life and the guide he provides to support others in living as mystics in everyday life, see the following by Aquinata Böckmann, OSB: "The Experience of God in the Rule of St. Benedict," *Benedictines* 51, no. 2 (Winter, 1998), 6–19; "Benedictine Mysticism: Dynamic Spirituality in the Rule of Benedict," trans. Eric Raymond, OSB, *Tjurunga* 57 (1999): 85–101.

14. Thornton Wilder, *Our Town* (New York: Perennial of HarperCollins, 2003), 94–109.

15. John O'Donohue, "A Blessing," in *Eternal Echoes: Exploring Our Yearning to Belong,* (New York: HarperCollins, 1999), 97.

Bibliography

Bass, Dorothy. *Receiving the Day: Christian Practices for Opening the Gift of Time*. San Francisco: Jossey-Bass, 2000.

Berg, Elizabeth. *Talk Before Sleep*. New York: Random House, 1994.

Bondi, Roberta. *Memories of God: Theological Reflections on a Life*. Nashville: Abdingdon Press, 1995.

Brown, Barbara Taylor. *An Altar in the World: A Geography of Faith*. New York: HarperOne, 2009.

Casey, Michael, OCSO. *A Guide to Living in the Truth: Saint Benedict's Teaching on Humility*. Liguori, MO: Liguori/Triumph, 2001.

———. *Strangers to the City: Reflections on the Beliefs and Values of the Rule of Saint Benedict*. Brewster, MA: Paraclete Press, 2005.

———. *An Unexciting Life: Reflections on Benedictine Spirituality*. Petersham, MA: St. Bede's Publications, 2005.

Chittister, Joan. *Wisdom Distilled from the Daily: Living the Rule of St. Benedict Today*. San Francisco: HarperSanFrancisco, 1991.

———, and Rowan Williams. *Uncommon Gratitude: Alleluia for All That Is*. Collegeville, MN: Liturgical Press, 2010.

Cummings, Charles, OCSO. *Monastic Practices*. Kalamazoo: Cistercian Publications, 1986.

De Waal, Esther. *Seeking God: The Way of St. Benedict*. Collegeville, MN: Liturgical Press, 2001.

———. *Seeking Life: The Baptismal Invitation of the Rule of St. Benedict*. Collegeville, MN: Liturgical Press, 2009.

Dorr, Donal. *Spirituality: Our Deepest Heart's Desire*. Blackrock, Ireland: Columba Press, 2009.

———. *Spirituality and Justice*. Maryknoll, NY: Orbis Books, 1984.

Dumm, Demetrius, OSB. *Flowers in the Desert: A Spirituality of the Bible*. New York: Paulist Press, 1987.

Farrington, Debra K. *Hearing with the Heart: A Gentle Guide to Discerning God's Will for Your Life*. San Francisco: Jossey-Bass, 2003.

Gruen, Anseln. *Heaven Begins Within You: Wisdom from the Desert Fathers.* Translated by Peter Heinegg. New York: Crossroad, 1994.

Guenther, Margaret. *Just Passing Through: Notes from a Sojourner.* New York: Church Publishing, 2007.

Hall, Jeremy, OSB. *Silence, Solitude, Simplicity: A Hermit's Love Affair with a Noisy, Crowded, and Complicated World.* Collegeville, MN: Liturgical Press, 2007.

Hanh, Thich Nhat. *The Miracle of Mindfulness.* Boston: Beacon Press, 1976.

Hart, Thomas N. *The Art of Christian Listening.* Mahwah, NJ: Paulist Press, 1980.

Henry, Patrick. *The Ironic Christian's Companion: Finding the Marks of God's Grace in the World.* New York: Riverhead Books, 1999.

Homan, Daniel, OSB, and Lonni Collins Pratt. *Radical Hospitality: Benedict's Way of Love.* Paraclete Press, 2002.

Howard, Katherine, OSB. *Praying with Benedict.* Winona: Saint Mary's Press, Christian Brothers Publication, 1996.

Jones, John Miriam, SC. *With An Eagle's Eye: A Seven-day Sojourn in Celtic Spirituality.* Notre Dame, IN: Ave Maria Press, 1998.

Kidd, Sue Monk. *The Secret Life of Bees.* New York: Penguin, 2003.

Lewis, Larry, MM. *The Misfit: Haunting the Human Unveiling the Divine.* Maryknoll, NY: Orbis Books, 1997.

Livingston, Patricia. *Let in the Light: Facing the Hard Stuff with Hope.* Notre Dame, IN: Sorin Books, 2006.

Nouwen, Henri. *Reaching Out: The Three Movements of the Spiritual Life.* Garden City, NY: Doubleday, 1975, chapters 4–6.

Pohl, Christine D. *Making Room: Recovering Hospitality as a Christian Tradition.* Grand Rapids, MI: Eerdmans, 1999.

Quindlen, Anna. *One True Thing.* New York: Random House, 1994.

Remen, Rachel. *My Grandfather's Blessings: Stories, Strength, and Belonging.* New York: Riverhead Books, 2000.

Reuter, Mary, OSB. "A Second Look: Mysticism in Everyday Life." *Studies in Formative Spirituality,* 5, no. 1 (February, 1984): 81–93.

———. "Time on our Hands, Time in Our Hearts." *Review for Religious* 45, no. 2 (March-April, 1986): 256–265.

Rolheiser, Ronald, OMI. *The Holy Longing: The Search for a Christian Spirituality.* New York: Doubleday, 1999.

Sanders, Scott Russell. *The Force of Spirit.* Boston: Beacon Press, 2000.

———. "Honoring the Ordinary." *Arts & Letters,* no. 18 (Fall 2007): 160–174.

———. "A Private History of Awe." *Orion Magazine* (Jan. 03), 52–58.

Schmidt, Joseph, FSC. *Praying Our Experiences*. Ijamsville, MD: The Word Among Us Press, 2008.

Steere, Douglas. *On Being Present Where You Are*. Lebanon, PA: Pendle Hills Publications, 1967.

Stewart, Columba, OSB. *Prayer and Community: The Benedictine Tradition*. Maryknoll, NY: Orbis Books, 1998.

Sultenfuss, Sylvia. *The Joy of Adulthood: A Crash Course in Designing the Life You Want*. Atlanta: Palladium Productions, 2004.

Swander, Mary. *Desert Pilgrim: Enroute to Mysticism and Miracles*. New York: Compass Press, 2003.

Taylor, John. *The Go-Between God: The Holy Spirit and the Christian Mission*. New York: Oxford University Press, 1972.

Wagner, Mary Anthony, OSB. *The Sacred World of the Christian: Sensed in Faith*. Collegeville, MN: Liturgical Press, 1993.

Wiederkehr, Macrina, OS.B. *A Tree Full of Angels: See the Holy in the Ordinary*. San Francisco: Harper and Row, 1988.

Wolf, Molly. *Hiding in Plain Sight: Sabbath Blessings*. Collegeville, MN: Liturgical Press, 1998.